SRI M, yogi and global spiritual guide, is an author, social reformer and educationist. He had secretly left his Kerala home at the age of nineteen to search for a yogi in the far-off Himalayas, and met his guru, Sri Maheshwarnath Babaji. His autobiography, *Apprenticed to a Himalayan Master*, is the astonishing story of how a Muslim boy from Kerala became an influential Hindu yogi and international spiritual teacher. The book became an instant bestseller when published in 2011. Its sequel, *The Journey Continues*, appeared in 2017. Babaji initiated him into kriya yoga and Vedanta, and he was taught other religious traditions too. Sri M's books on philosophy and mysticism include Wisdom of the Rishis and Yoga is also for the Godless. His epic Walk of Hope in 2015–16 covered 7,500 miles from the southernmost tip of India to Kashmir in the north, and it took him sixteen months to complete it. Sri M established The Satsang Foundation in Madanapalle twenty years ago and runs free schools for underprivileged children, community health care centres and does COVID-19 relief work, tree planting and other projects. He has received many honours and awards, including the prestigious Padma Bhushan from the Indian Government for service of high order in the field of spirituality.

Mohini Kent, Lady Noon, is an author, film-maker, journalist and charity worker. Her books include *Black Taj*, *Nagarjuna: The Second Buddha* (on Buddhist philosophy) and *Dear Mama*, a collection of intimate letters from eminent persons to their own mothers. She wrote and directed *The Ramayana* feature film as well as *Curry Tiffin*, a documentary on the history of India through food, and worked with Sir Ben Kingsley on both films. Her stage plays include *Rumi: Unveil the Sun*, on the Sufi mystic Mevlana Rumi, done in collaboration with her mother, Amrit Kent. She has written for several news magazines, including *India Today*, *Sunday Times*, *The Week*, and had her own fortnightly slot on *BBC Radio*. She gives public talks on women's causes, food, charity, and mentoring talks to the youth. She is widely read in Western and Indian literature and philosophy, including ancient and modern spiritual teachings. She is the Global Envoy of the International Buddhist Confederation (IBC) in the UK as well as a Founder Chairperson of the charity Lily Against Human Trafficking, which works against the trade in human beings, with a focus on abused children. She lives between Delhi and London.

ADVANCE PRAISE FOR THE BOOK

'In these insightful interviews with Sri M conducted over more than a year in different locations, Mohini Kent offers a deeply moving account of his life, influences and thoughts on a wide variety of subjects including yoga, friendship, sex, marriage and power. Baroness Kent is herself a seeker interested in living a life of truth and integrity and her questions spring from the challenges she has encountered. As a result, they have a depth and existential immediacy and lead Sri M to respond at the appropriate level. The interviews present both at their most reflective and make this a helpful guide to life. Sri M's countless followers owe his interlocutor a deep sense of gratitude.'

—Lord Prof. Bhikhu Parekh,
Member of House of Lords, UK

'It is always a pleasure to read Sri M because of his clarity and spiritual articulation. Mohini Kent, herself a well established author, has evoked fascinating responses by her intelligent questioning; a truly meaningful conversation.'

—Dr Karan Singh

THE
FRIEND

SRI M

with

MOHINI KENT

PENGUIN BOOKS

An imprint of Penguin Random House

PENGUIN BOOKS

USA | Canada | UK | Ireland | Australia
New Zealand | India | South Africa | China

Penguin Books is part of the Penguin Random House group of companies
whose addresses can be found at global.penguinrandomhouse.com

Published by Penguin Random House India Pvt. Ltd
4th Floor, Capital Tower 1, MG Road,
Gurugram 122 002, Haryana, India

Penguin
Random House
India

First published in Penguin Books by Penguin Random House India 2022

ISBN 9780143457169

Typeset in Adobe Garamond Pro by Manipal Technologies Limited, Manipal
Printed at Replika Press Pvt. Ltd, India

www.penguin.co.in

Yesterday I was clever, so I wanted to change the world. Today I am wise, so I am changing myself.—Mevlana Rumi (Sufi Mystic, 1207–1273 CE)

The happiness of your life depends upon the quality of your thoughts; therefore take care that you entertain no notions unsuitable to virtue and reasonable nature. —Marcus Aurelius (Roman emperor, 161–180 CE)

A calm and modest life brings more happiness than the pursuit of success combined with constant restlessness.—Albert Einstein (German born physicist, 1879–1955 CE)

Life is like a butter lamp fluttering in a strong wind (it can be snuffed out any moment).—Nagarjuna, also called The Second Buddha (circa 150–250 CE)

The unexamined life is not worth living.—Socrates (Greek philosopher, 470–399 BCE)

Contents

Preface

I am honoured to offer this short and simple book of Sri M's quintessential wisdom to my fellow travellers on the path to illumination. It touches upon many essential subjects, both temporal and causal, material and esoteric. Like sunlight scattering gold coins on the heaving waters of the sea, the world dazzles us, but the origin of the gold lies elsewhere.

It was Sri M's astonishing autobiography that sparked off in me the desire to seek him out, to meet an authentic yogi from the great spiritual lineage of the Nath Panth, tracing its origin back to Adi Nath, the first Nath. His narrative about his incredible journey is unpretentious and accessible, and clearly laid out in his book, *Apprenticed to a Himalayan Master.*

I travelled to Madanapalle on 1 August 2016. We had earlier met briefly when he was in Delhi on his epic Walk of Hope. It was a hot summer's day in August and the road up from Bengaluru airport was lined with soaring coconut palms and supari trees, and the hills of naked rocks piled up high that look stunning in the southern landscape. At Sri M's ashram, I was surprised to learn that he would arrive the next day specially to meet me. While spiritual relationships are traditionally a two-way link, our internet age has created a weird familiarity without actual physical contact; so it impressed me that he made time for a personal meeting. Meanwhile, I watched small children from nearby tribal communities walk up in their rubber slippers to attend Sri M's free school. They grinned and waved and practised their entire vocabulary of English words on me.

For me, 2016 was yet another difficult year. I felt empty and frozen inside and hoped to get some answers from Sri M. We met the next morning. He was welcoming but I felt he was assessing me, as if he was marking my report card. He met me again that evening. That night, I felt the first flicker of happiness in my deadened heart after a long time.

Life is unexpected and I was always adventurous. That is fine as long as the experiences are pleasant, but being a young woman from Delhi alone in London—displaced in a foreign society—made the situation very tricky for me. I faced blistering challenges and learnt tough lessons about identity, livelihood and money, and met many 'hungry ghosts'. A hungry ghost in Hinduism is a preta, demonic undead creature. The Japanese call them *gaki*. Hungry ghosts also live among us in the shape of men and women, endlessly gobbling things and people. Hungry ghosts had oppressed me, pushing me to the verge of a breakdown, and I went to Sri M seeking succour. He lifted a heavy burden off me and said, 'All that did not happen by chance. Your soul chose the hard learning, but now you are free. Don't compromise your freedom. That's the only thing that will help you in the end'.

The worldly challenges I faced were made worse by the constant existential refrain which had bothered me from a young age: Why? When? Who? Why am I here on earth? When will I understand the purpose of life? Who can tell me that? Some of my own reflections—mirroring the same existential angst that others suffer from—are also a part of this book.

As I became better acquainted with Sri M, I began to appreciate his openness. He is not restrictive. 'Accept Divine help from wherever you get it', he said.

My conversations with him took place over 2019 and 2020 in Delhi, London, Banaras and Madanapalle. We talked for an hour each time. I further took the opportunity to ask additional questions in our several public online conversations during the COVID-19 pandemic.

Sri M is always frank and direct in his responses, not given to answering through baffling hints or cryptic comments, and he does not hesitate to say 'I don't know'.

He delivers great teachings with a light touch, easily digestible, and always punctuated by humour. I have watched him patiently and carefully answer questions at public satsangs, even if the query sounded inane or superfluous. His presence is joyful, and he is a living exemplar of inner freedom.

The title of this book, *The Friend*, suggested itself quite naturally, and is a reflection of his own personality as well as his approach. He says, 'I have to make friends with someone before I can guide them.'

I have structured the book in such a way so as to create a natural progression from Sri M's personal reflections on his own beloved guru to his teachings on more wide-ranging topics such as love, sex, power, wealth, marriage, women's equality, friendship, food, children, breath, death, yoga, liberation, aspects of ancient wisdom, the spiritual path, the Upanishads, the pandemic, the youth, the spinning wheel of existence that propels us into the future. No subject was off limits.

I share this book of Sri M's teachings with all those who seek to go beyond the deadening march of humdrum days, the endless demands of the wallet, the prison of the mind, and the chains that bind us to relationships, to our own expectations, and to society. It is a map to the nugget of pure gold within us, and the map can as easily be followed by a novice as by more seasoned travellers on the path. Sri M assures us that liberation is available to all, and is not only for the select few, but to attain it we must do our own homework.

He urges us to embark on the journey now, without delay, in order to reclaim the free and joyous beings that we truly are.

Lady Mohini Kent Noon
London 2022
Founder Chairperson of the charity
LILY Against Human Trafficking
Global Envoy in the UK of the
International Buddhist Confederation (IBC)

About Sri M

Sri M's spiritual journey started at the age of nine when his guru came to him. Thus began a period of intense transformation for the boy during which he received visions in dreams, met a number of spiritual saints and teachers, Hindus, Muslims, Brahmins, Sufis, men and women from all religions, who gave him spiritual gifts. He experienced rapid inner growth that irresistibly impelled him to leave home a decade later in search of the truth. His was an affluent Kerala family and, as the eldest son, he received all the possible attention; but he slipped away quietly at the age of nineteen, without a word to anybody and left for the unknown Himalayas, 2000 miles away from his native place. Ever since he was a child he had yearned for the mountains, imagined snow-clad peaks in place of the banks of white clouds he beheld above him, and now he was bound for them, to seek out a yogi, he knew not who.

After a few adventurous months spent wandering in Haridwar, Rishikesh, and Badrinath—sleeping rough and starving at times, with burnt and blistered feet, but also being sheltered in temples, ashrams, and meeting some remarkable saints—he had still not found his Himalayan yogi. He got lost in the thick forests near Rudraprayag, spent hours contemplating the clear waters of the holy river Ganges in silvery moonlight, encountered great scholars, experts on yoga, ganja-smoking Naga sadhus, but was not satisfied. Something drove him to carry on climbing the mountain ranges ever higher. On a cold autumn night, he had climbed past Mana (the last village in India) and Vyas Cave, which was dark and deserted. Assailed by doubt and despair, he contemplated suicide by throwing himself into the freezing waters of the Alaknanda River far down below, but his search was almost at an end. On his way down, he saw a fire blazing outside Vyas Cave, and heard a voice call out 'Madhu', telling him to come inside. The voice belonged to Sri Maheshwarnath Babaji, his guru, who had first come to him at the age of nine.

For almost four years, Sri M wandered with his guru in the trackless mountains, being initiated, tutored and carefully nurtured by him. It was a life unlike any he had known—living in Himalayan caves, walking on pilgrimage to holy sites, visiting the hidden valley of flowers, gaining insights from other saints of different faiths, crossing into Tibet, being initiated into the Nath

Panth—and all the while being instructed and readied for his mission to come.

At the end of the period, Babaji asked him to return to his parents, to the world, get married and lead a normal life, and to bide his time until his guru gave him the signal to embark on his spiritual mission. His mother, who loved him dearly and would have willingly sacrificed anything for his happiness, accepted him back without any fuss. He writes about her: 'The mother who welcomed me after years with not a word of protest when I came back a wandering yogi, far from the religion she and I were born into. Only a mother can do this.' He adds that Mother is also the universal principle of motherhood that bestows compassion and grace on all beings.

Sri M, spiritual guru, social reformer, activist and author, is now a beloved guide to many people, and travels widely from his base in Madanapalle, India. In 2015–16, he led an epic walk up the length of India for communal harmony, from the southernmost tip of India to Kashmir in the north. He has written several books apart from his autobiography, including *On Meditation*, *Wisdom of the Rishis*, *Jewel in the Lotus*, *Yoga is also for the Godless*, *Shunya*, a novel, and a book of short stories, *Homecoming*.

In tandem with his spiritual mission is Sri M's active compassion in his social work to uplift the dispossessed. His Satsang Foundation initiates and manages humanitarian projects such as a free school for the children of tribal communities living in and around Madanapalle (the children I noticed on my first visit). Such children would otherwise face a future as goatherds and itinerant vegetable vendors, much as what their mothers and fathers do. The foundation also runs a free clinic for those communities, giving healthcare to people who would have had patchy medical attention at best. During the hunger crisis of 2020 that was created by the chaos of the pandemic, volunteers of the Satsang Foundation distributed food in several Indian cities over several months to starving adults and children.

A modern guru for modern times, Sri M demonstrates how to live in the teeming world, do our spiritual practices, be of service to others and become agents of change for good. Rooted in the ancient wisdom of Vedanta, he also assimilated the truth of other paths, as directed by his guru. The broad base of his vision, knowledge and understanding of different traditions, his spontaneity and simplicity, make him much admired and in great demand. Sri M left home in search of the truth, spent his youth wandering with his guru in the icy Himalayas, and now traverses the globe sharing those teachings with people of different nationalities, cultures and beliefs.

On the Guide and the Way

My Guru

Q: You have spoken often and affectionately about the years spent with your guru Maheshwarnath Babaji. Is such a strong bond of trust and love rare, or can we all hope to find it in our lives? What did your guru truly mean to you?

My master, Maheshwarnath Babaji, was my father, my mother, my guru, my teacher, my friend, everything rolled into one. He was a great yogi who had transcended form, but he kept his body very young and fit for a purpose. He was very tall, and extremely fair. When he told me to give him a hug, I came up to his shoulders.

I have never met anyone else like him on this earth. He looked about thirty. I was about twenty then, and some people thought I was his younger brother. Later, I aged, but he did not. Some people would come to meet him whose families had known him for generations, and they

1

said he had always looked the same. He may have lived for 200 years. One lady, a grandmother, said she had met him as a young girl because he had been friendly with her own grandfather, and he still looked exactly the same.

He was knowledgeable about all traditions and various scriptures. It was all there in his head. Once I asked him about a text I wanted to read. He concentrated for a moment and told me it was kept in a temple library in south India, written on palm leaf. We were up in the Himalayas. When I insisted that I wanted to study it, he told me to come back in a couple of hours and sat down in concentration. Two hours later he dictated it to me, chapter by chapter.

All knowledge was available to him through meditation and understanding. He would remain quiet and get the answer, and he gave me the key to the library within him.

The role of a guru is to wake you up. Babaji taught me that there should be eternal watchfulness. It is not easy.

Q: Babaji trained you in so many different traditions, or he sent you to others to be trained. Why do you think that was so? Could he have foreseen how, later, you would be travelling around the globe?

Babaji had the spiritual capacity to see it all. He caught my thoughts even before they occurred to me.

He wanted me to study Christianity. 'Suppose in future you need to talk to a bishop?' he asked. 'What bishop? Where?' I countered. We were up in the Himalayas and there was no one round for miles. In Dallas, I have installed the image of Mary. I said to myself that I have to bring in the Shakti and in this country that is Mother Mary, so I invoked the Presence.

I learnt many things just by listening to Babaji, and he would make me understand in so many different ways. He trained me in Vedas, Upanishads, meditation and Kriya Yoga.[1] When we were camping in Mauni Baba's cave near Rishikesh, in the foothills of the Himalayas, his favourite place to teach me in the evenings was on the steps of an old ashram leading down to the river. The cave is still there. We would get a boat across the Ganges to the old ashram, watch the river flowing past and the people in their boats. Babaji had the entire Upanishads and other texts stored in his memory and could recite them at will. There seemed to be nothing he did not know. He could pick up languages by empathy and identity. I might think he would not know about this or that, but he always did.

He would also send me to others. He sent me to a Naga Baba who was naked and smoked a chillum with some form of cannabis. As his apprentice, I had to take off

---

[1] Kriya Yoga is an ancient spiritual technique for self-realization.

my clothes too and smoke. After two months, I pleaded with Babaji to call me back.

Babaji sent me to join the Gaudiya Math in Vrindavan. I took the *nama* and chanted the *nama*.[2] The Gaudiya Math came into existence many years after Chaitanya Mahaprabhu. Srila Prabhupada was from the Gaudiya Math. When Babaji came to take me back, he said, 'You've learnt what you had to, now let's go.'

He taught me that I must have a good character. Without that, other practices do not give results. So purify your *Yama Niyamas* first, follow the dos and the don'ts, the rules and regulations.

Q: What was it like to be with Babaji? What was his personality like?

Babaji was joyous, it was joyful to be with him, it was fun. But it can be painful when a teacher points out what you really are, not what you think you are. People don't like to face their weaknesses.

He could get angry with me, not real anger, but genuine concern, like when one worries about the welfare of a child. Then he would say, '*Chupp!*' Be quiet!

Whatever Babaji asked me to do, I did it, but I also used to argue with that great man with such immense

___
[2] *Nama* here is the Name of God. It is a Sanskrit term.

4

spiritual capacities. I was nineteen years old, a rebellious age, but he never discouraged me from asking questions. He was so normal, so kind and affectionate, he laughed and joked with me. He had a very direct, forthright and blunt way of speaking.

Babaji also had a terrific sense of humour. When it was time for him to quit his body, he summoned me to the Himalayas. By then, I was living in the plains. He said, 'It's good to leave the mother-in-law's house while you're still young.'

Q: How did you recognize your guru? With travel made easy today, we can meet a number of spiritual guides; so how is one to tell who is the right guru? Who is a true guru?

I had secretly left home to search for a yogi in the Himalayas. As a small child in Kerala, I looked at the clouds and imagined they were snow-capped mountains. After a couple of months in Rishikesh, I went up to Badrinath. It was cold. Then I went up further. I passed the Vyasa *gufa*, a cave, and there was nobody there. I was depressed. I was stumbling down on the way back, in the dark, but this time there was a fire, a *dhuni* burning in the mouth of the Vyasa cave. There was somebody there now. A tall man called me in. His eyes were the same as those of the man I had met when I was nine, when a stranger had appeared in the courtyard of our family home, under the jackfruit tree. The stranger had thickly matted long hair gathered on top of his head and large, brownish-black eyes overflowing with affection. His body was bare except for a white cloth wrapped around his middle, down to his knees. He had put his blessed hand on my head and asked if I remembered anything. I did not. He said I would understand later and sent me back indoors. My guru had come to me, and my spiritual journey had started.

Now I had found him again after a long search. I spontaneously called him Babaji, and I said, 'I will never leave you. I will stay with you forever.' 'We'll see', he replied. The next morning, he took me across the Ganges to his own cave in Charan Paduka. Babaji had no paraphernalia, no banner.

I also learnt to understand the relationship with a spiritual teacher, which is an intimate one between the teacher and the disciple. Once you start your spiritual journey, you are always on the teacher's radar.

After three and a half years of wandering with him in the mountains, he told me, 'Go home, have a normal life and help people using what you have learnt.'

I was the only son of the family, the eldest child, and suddenly at nineteen I had disappeared. My mother was suffering.

One day Babaji asked, 'Did you write a letter to your mother?'

I had not. 'If I write to them, they will know where I am and send somebody to take me back. Why don't you do something for her?' I said, mischievously.

After years, I saw my mother again. She later told me that she had had a dream in which a long-haired man with a white cloth across his waist had told her that I was fine. He had said, 'He's in my cave. He'll be back. Don't worry.' Not that my mother felt any better after that.

Get to know a teacher before you trust that person. Don't blindly accept a formula from anyone but examine it for yourself. Spend time and observe how that person behaves, both in public and in private. A simple criterion is to see if they want to give you something or take something from you.

Q: *Apart from the formal teachings of scriptures and the ancient wisdom of the rishis that Babaji gave you, what are the other important things you feel you imbibed from him?*

Babaji taught me to have great respect for nature. He repeated many times that the mountains, rivers and trees are our primary gods. He taught me to respect water and food, to conserve energy. To eat vegetarian food, because if you pluck an apple from a tree, the tree can grow other apples. But when you eat an animal, you finish one unit. From that animal would have come other animals. We must conserve energy, not waste it.

Find the right mind-body balance. There is an outer environment and an inner environment.

He said that it doesn't matter what people think of you, but if you begin to believe it about yourself then you are sunk. That applies to gurus too. Criticism balances the adulation. One has to watch oneself carefully.

The essential thing is to listen with a completely unprejudiced mind to one who has travelled on the path and touched the goal, with no old garbage cluttering up your head. That's very rare. I had read books on philosophy and religion in my university library by the time I met Babaji, and one year was spent on unloading and emptying myself. The preparation is to have space, to empty out prejudices, to be free. There needs to be space. That preparation can be done in any tradition.

Babaji taught me to seek reality. 'You never know the root of a thing when it happens', he said.

'What do you mean?' I asked. I was always asking questions.

He had an earthy sense of humour. 'OK listen. A man was walking along the bund of a paddy field. Suddenly he needed to defecate urgently, but you can't do that in a paddy field. If the villagers caught him, they would beat him up. But nature's call was urgent, so he sat on the bund and did his job. Just as he finished, he saw villagers walking towards him. What to do next? He quickly collected some mud and piled it on. Grabbing a hibiscus flower, he placed it on top and sat down in front of it in a prayerful attitude.

The villagers stopped and asked, "What are you doing?"

"This mound has just come up and I am worshipping it", he replied. The villagers joined him.'

In my novel, when Shunya departs, he leaves behind some excreta that they bury, then build a big structure on top.

The story of Shunya is partly about Babaji.

Q: Is there no other image of Babaji apart from your painting of him in your autobiography?

I wanted to have his photograph to keep with me, but he was against photography. It was only years after he had passed away, after he had told me to write my autobiography, that I could paint the portrait for my book. Babaji was fair like a European but the artist helping me with the book was a Krishna devotee, so he made him blue!

I lived with Babaji for over three years, and we often travelled. We even went to Tibet. Then he told me to go home. First, he sent me to a barber shop to cut my hair, saying, 'Don't go to your mother looking like that. And shave.'

Babaji also said, 'I'll keep in touch with you. When you need me, I'll be there.' He called me back many times, in strange ways. Sometimes I would feel a strong call within and go.

He told me to get married since most people who would come to me in the future would be married and I could not help or advise them if I did not know what married life was like.

Q: Why did Babaji quit this life? He never seemed to feel the cold, even up in the icy mountains, or need to eat or sleep like all human beings do.

Babaji did not eat to live. He would eat something if I brought it for him, and I remember taking him *langda*[3] mangoes from a field. But he looked after me and would ask me to fetch vegetables and learn how to cook. He told me to take only what I could eat and keep a little aside to feed other creatures.

It is true Babaji never felt cold or hungry. I never saw him sleep. He did not wear footwear but always walked barefoot, even in winter in the Himalayas. On the frozen Gangotri glacier, he did not use even a blanket. But he looked after me, gave me blankets and told me to cover my ears. I think he had practiced Tummo[4] in his early

---

[3] Mango grown in Uttar Pradesh, Northern India.

[4] Tummo is a tantric practice for inner heat, developed round the concept of the female deity.

days and could heat up his body. The ancient meditation technique originated in the Himalayas and is used by Buddhist monks. I was intrigued and wanted to learn it.

He replied, in his usual forthright way, 'I can teach you Tummo, but there's no need. Instead of spending five years mastering Tummo, you can buy a shawl for five rupees.' But he did teach me the technique, which has to do with the Manipur Chakra, its *beej akshara*[5] and there are many other things in it as well. Years of practise will heat up the body.

Why did he leave his body? I think he had had enough. No other problem. He had no illness, not even the hint of old age. It's just that he decided to leave the earth plane. In April 1985, he contacted me through a sadhu who told me in Chennai that Babaji was calling me to Rishikesh. I left immediately, went there and headed straight for Mauni Baba's cave.

Babaji told me, 'It's time to go. I have done my work. I have somebody else to do the work now.'

He went in the most extraordinary way. He gave me instructions in the finer points of *kriya* practice and what to do with his body once he had abandoned it, and for that I had to dig a pit of certain dimensions.

---

[5] One-syllable sounds that are meant to activate the chakras along the centre line of the body, or the seven main chakras.

Then he sat down in padmaasana[6] breathed in, breathed out vigorously a few times. His eyes were fixed on the centre of his forehead. After one last vigorous exhalation, he was gone.

Babaji left me with certain responsibilities to teach and guide. That was my guru's directive, and there is a lot of work to be done.

---

[6] Padmaasana or Lotus pose is a cross-legged yoga posture which makes the body stable in meditation. Buddha is depicted as seated in Padmaasana.

The Teacher

Q: So many teachings from various traditions are widely available in books all over the world, and freely available on the internet. Is it essential to have a living spiritual guide or teacher, or can one do it alone?

There's nothing better than a good teacher. The law of spiritual life is that the sincere aspirant will find the right guidance on the path. But first you must have the burning desire for spiritual fulfilment, not matter what it takes. The spiritual path is not for window shoppers. It requires hard work and persistent effort. Everyone slogs for money, but how many want to work hard for spiritual attainment?

The teacher is important. It's good to get guidance to walk on uncharted territory, unexplored landscapes, from someone who has walked on the path and can say, 'Watch out! *This* is better', or '*that* is better'. But each one has to walk on the path. You must begin the journey by assuming you know nothing. Get rid of the load you are carrying, the notion that you already know everything. First wipe the slate clean.

When you do meet someone who has enjoyed the journey, then you will understand the beauty of it, and how wonderful it is. The spiritual path does not mean walking round with a frown on your face or not wearing good clothes, for you cannot isolate yourself from this world.

It just means your mind is looking for 'that' wherever you are. It is a continuous journey.

Very few great beings have existed who have had no obvious personal teacher, but these very mature souls manifested only after many lives with many teachers.

Q: If one does identify the right teacher and the right path, then at what point does it become unquestioning allegiance? Is faith blind?

Faith means to first put faith in yourself, and then put faith in the one whom you feel confident could guide you. Faith is like a hypothesis, and then you must discover for yourself if is true or not. But at least accept the hypothesis that there is spirituality, and there are ways and means to reach there. If you don't accept the hypothesis and take the first step with faith, how will you ever arrive?

A great teacher will not want you to be dependent upon him or her. The teachings are more important than the teacher and must be practised. You need to study and practise and practise. One of Patanjali's most important directives is 'regular and continuous practise'. Don't expect to get results if you are not practising.

If someone claims to be a spiritual guru but is upset by criticism, then where does he stand? Ask yourself if he is tranquil in the face of temptations, pain and sorrow, joy and happiness, praise and blame. Has his, or her, mind become settled? *Stitha pragnya*. Is he, or she, interested in your cheque book, are they kind to the rich and indifferent to the poor? Then you will have your answer.

If even after all that you jump to the wrong conclusion, ask yourself what lesson you need to learn from that, and then move on to identify the right guide.

When I meet someone, I say to myself, 'There is in me a spark of the divine, and it is in that person too, and I won't look at anything else.' That is a good basis for a relationship. All negativity then falls away and we learn to see the good. But if you see only negative things, then harmony is impossible. Unhappy people have their own pressures which have nothing to do with us—it could be a bad boss or an unhappy marriage.

Each person is a spark of the divine. There's no such thing as 'a common man'. What we all have in common is the capacity to search for the Truth. Ultimately, you are your own master. My job is to tell you that your teacher is in you. A good teacher can help you understand that, and if you do grasp that then you are free.

Q: Can a good guide help one pick up speed in one's spiritual evolution? And what about the emotional bond with the teacher? We are all looking for reassurance from somebody else.

A good disciple is as hard to find as a good teacher, and one must learn how to become a good disciple. Once a man went to a guru and asked to become his disciple. The guru accepted him. He was given the task of looking after the ashram, which meant rising early every morning to clean the hut, fetch water from the river Ganges, collect wood for the *dhuni* and other tasks. The disciple did not like that. 'What is needed to become a guru?' he asked. The reply was 'You have to sit in padmaasana and say, "God bless you" with your hand raised.' The man was happy and said, 'Then make me guru.'

Only a mature mind, one who has experienced a lot and understood it, is capable of that real search. One of the great disciples of Chaitanya Mahaprabhu was a Muslim named Haridas. Even before he met Chaitanya, Haridas went around Mayapur chanting '*Hare Krishna*'. The story goes that there is not a single place in Mayapur or Puri where Haridas had not bowed his head to Krishna, and he chanted Krishna's name till the day he died. When he met Chaitanya, he became his disciple even though he was older. Chaitanya settled in Puri twenty-four years before he died. Haridas was not allowed to enter the Puri temple because he was Muslim, but he had built himself a small hut at the corner of the temple's outer wall. Chaitanya would visit the temple daily and emerge singing and dancing in ecstasy, and Haridas would be waiting for him. Chaitanya Mahaprabhu would hug him, causing Haridas to exclaim, 'Now I have Puri Jagannath with me.'

Then Haridas fell seriously ill and could not even rise up from the floor of his hut where he lay. Chaitanya went to visit him straight after darshan at the temple, and, as usual, he was in a state of ecstasy. Haridas saw Chaitanya and cried, 'Now I can go to Vaikuntha. Please place your feet on my chest.' Chaitanya sat down and gently placed his feet on Haridas' chest. Haridas hugged those precious feet, closed his eyes, repeated '*Hari! Hari!*' twice and died. There have been some wonderful people.

One must learn to first become a disciple before becoming a master.

The bond between a guru and a sincere disciple is a very close one. The guru accepts the consciousness of the disciple into his own sphere of influence, so that he can be aware of the activities, thoughts and feelings of the disciple.

The Company You Keep

Q: Why is keeping good company so important? You have laid stress upon the value of satsang, even if it is between two people.

Satsang is very important because you become like the company you keep. If you live with people who talk about truth, seek truth, who do *nama japa*,[7] kirtan[8] and bhajan, you will become like them after some time. Then another faculty will open up called the opening of the 'Heart'. Not the anatomical heart, but a faculty called the '*Hridaya Chakra*', and that opens up affection, compassion, love and devotion.

Religions may differ in their philosophies, but all of them profess to give the same message, that a human being should become kind and loving. Being compassionate towards all living beings is a virtue central to all faiths and don't forget about yourself because, more often than not, we are unkind to our own self, more than to anyone else.

Your sadhana[9] is very important, and that is what a guru wants. If we are close to one whom we consider to be a great teacher, and worship him for years, but remain the same angry, selfish, greedy, petty person as before, then all

---

[7] *Nama Japa* or *Nama Sankeertanam* is the *japa* (repetition) or *Sankirtana* of *nama* (name) of the Almighty.
[8] A devotional song in which a group repeats lines sung by a leader.
[9] Disciplined and dedicated practise or learning, especially in religion.

that sadhana comes to naught. There are highly evolved souls who did not have to do much sadhana, at least not in this lifetime, but did it in order to set an example to others to observe and learn.

You need infinite patience in sadhana, for sorrows, trials and tribulations are part of life from the moment we are born. Do not be discouraged, just bear with it and stay with the process. No one can ever expect to be totally free of material problems in this world, so don't wait to first put things right. Stick to your sadhana and do your meditation. Things will take care of themselves. Go through the tests, pass them and move forward in your spiritual life. No one can say exactly when the grace of God will arrive.

On Body and Mind

The Body

Q: Some traditions deny the importance of the body and our material existence on earth. Instead, they emphasize other, invisible realms such as paradise and purgatory. Where does the truth lie?

You are Spirit, but you are also the body. Without your physicality there is no progress, so your body must be cherished.

Each person has a different rate of metabolism. In old age, catabolism accelerates due to eating the wrong food, no exercise or too much exercise, all of which impact the cells. Toxins build up in the body and slow down the anabolism. It is recommended that every three to six months you do a cleansing process and free yourself of toxins, at least for the time being. Your metabolic rate will improve. That creates youthful energy and a youthful appearance. Appearance also depends on how you treat your body.

Disease arises in the stomach. We eat too many foods that add empty calories without giving us strength. The first step is to get your stomach cleansed, perhaps once every three months.

Your inner strength will also increase, and that will reflect in your cells. The endocrine system plays a great role in maintaining health and youthfulness. There are yoga asanas to keep your endocrine system alive. Walk. Keep active. I started practising yoga asanas at the age of eight or so and do asanas every day unless I am not well.

Cleansing also means that toxins can be eliminated through sweat. Take occasional warm water baths to help you sweat. Take an oil bath once a week, where you oil your body for an hour. Certain herbs are also helpful. Taking Chyawanprash[1] helps and having Triphala Churna[2] in the morning and evening helps keep your stomach clean. Constipation is one of the worst offenders.

Drink water before meals and not after meals. Avoid eating too much non-vegetarian food. Air your home, keep it well-ventilated. Spend some time walking among trees, breathing in fresh air. Eat less at night before sleeping.

---

[1] An Ayurvedic Rasayana which helps to boost immunity and physical well-being.

[2] Triphala Churna is an ayurvedic product, beneficial in vision related troubles, constipation and stomach problems.

Secret of Youthfulness

Q: In the age in which we live people are obsessed with youth. How does one keep youthful?

Youth is also a quality of the mind. Learn to see things in a new light. Allow the new rays to come in. That is as important as physical age.

While there is physical wear and tear, people also grow old because of abusing their bodies—too much food, too much drink, too much activity which is not necessary, too much worry and depression, all of which have an impact on physical ageing.

The condition of the mind and the body are interrelated. A mind that remains open remains young, and the vibration reaches every cell. Then the body also gets recharged.

Fifteen years ago, I was in a mould where I felt the best thing to do was to meditate and be quiet. Then it struck me that I must travel. Babaji had told me, 'You have to impart the knowledge.' He had also said that inconvenience is not an excuse, and I did feel that travelling would be inconvenient. Such opinions get stuck inside us, become rock-hard and interfere with the free flow of energy. In the beginning, it was a bit difficult with jet lag and other issues, but I changed at that point. It's never too late to change, but the change must first come in the mind. You can change until the very end, even on the deathbed. At any moment you should be able to break the old mould.

Do your homework. Combine that with your daily life. Some are old when still young, which means they don't move forward or receive fresh air. They are caught up in the pattern into which they were moulded, and do not want to break free. They stop learning. True, you cannot live without your own theory of life, your own concepts, but you should be open to breaking your own mould. When that happens, the body also gets recharged.

Q: How can we assist the process of renewal of cells in the body?

Physically and chemically, there are some natural medicines by which parts of your body can be improved. But the real feeling of youth and energy come when there are cellular changes. The rishis felt that one human lifetime is too short to attain liberation, so they created the knowledge and practice of Kaya Kalpa in Ayurveda.

The Hindu system is a science of body, mind and the evolutionary process of nature. Apart from the world we can see and touch, there are other dimensions of human existence which need to be explored. We need to consciously open up those parts of the brain neglected in the pursuit of external objects.

Q: You mentioned the ayurvedic system of Kaya Kalpa. What is that?

Kaya Kalpa is the study of the science of ageing. It aims to renew the cells at certain intervals of time in order to have a healthier life to attain the goal of moksha. Liberation. It is not possible to completely renew all the cells, but the majority can be stopped from decaying.

Kaya Kalpa is designed to enhance life, both its length and health. The system uses special foods, exercises and medicines, although Ayurveda *aushadhas*[3] cannot be described as medicine. The physical body is a stepping stone to finding something higher. If you don't have a strong and healthy physical body, you cannot have a healthy mind.

The system was not invented for the cosmetics industry. Beauty is relative. We should not use our standards of beauty to judge somebody else.

Q: Is it possible for a physical transformation of the body? Not only longevity, but actual transformation of the cellular consciousness?

Without a little bit of change at least in the cellular consciousness it is not possible to do Kaya Kalpa.

---

[3] Sanskrit term used in Ayurveda, roughly meaning 'made of herbs', 'medicinal herb', 'remedy', 'drug' or 'medicine'.

One of the things in Kaya Kalpa is to activate at least a couple of chakras in your system. All the centres from which energy flows into your system must be cleaned up and active. Some of the chakras, such as *Vishuddhi* (throat), *Manipura* (solar plexus) and *Mooladhara* (base chakra), need to be activated for Kaya Kalpa to be effective.

Yoga includes physical yoga and the quest to find the divine in one's life. When the heart and mind become soaked with the divine, the body expresses it by becoming refined and beautiful. Then everything is in harmony, in symmetry with all other parts. Even the cells undergo a change and you'll be surprised how much energy is available to you when you touch the source or touch the tap next to the source. There's tremendous energy available to be absorbed.

Yoga Is for All

Q: Yoga has become a buzzword today. The ancient science of yoga has spread from India to the rest of the world, and we have fashionable yoga studios, celebrity followers, hot and cold yoga, wheels of yoga, perhaps even black & white yoga. What is it actually, at its true yogic core?

Yoga is a technique which brings about changes in one's being, because of which one can understand the truth explained in the Upanishads that you are complete, *Poorna*. Don't hypnotize yourself into believing in your limitations.

Yoga is not otherworldly philosophy. It is meant for the here and now and offers a practical way of living in the world. The ancient rishis had done a deep study of yoga. They understood that there could be different types of yoga and they divided the theory and practice into different heads. They gave different names to the various forms of yoga such as Bhakti yoga, Gyan yoga and Karma yoga. The ideal is a synthesis of all these, but each person is built differently.

Patanjali put together the ancient science of yoga together for us. He refers to it as kriya yoga and it has eight parts, eight limbs, but he did not call it ashtanga yoga. The *Yoga Sutras* of Patanjali form the most concise and standard textbook. Commentaries are needed to understand each Sutra, and Vyasa's commentary on the *Yoga Sutras* is an important one.

The *Yoga Sutras* begin by defining it as *Chitt Vritti Nirodh*.[4] Yoga means overcoming the conflicts and instabilities of the mind. The mind is always moving about here and there, happy and sad, like a roller coaster. Yoga is a step-by-step process, if one truly practices it systematically, to reach a certain point where the mind is free of all distractions and tensions. *Yama* and *Niyama*, rules and regulations, have to be followed by one who strives to silence the mind.

For anything spiritual to happen you need to have a tranquil mind, free of fluctuations. The yogic mind is tranquil and quiet but very alert. Intelligence works one-pointedly but sees everything. In a yogi, all senses work equally well. It comes through practise, regular and incessant practise. There are no shortcuts.

It starts with asanas and pranayama. One must practice a few asanas and some breathing techniques. Very few people know how to breathe properly. They do shallow breathing. Practise pranayama to strengthen lungs and hold oxygen for a long time. If you can do proper yogic breathing, you can keep the cells and bronchial tubes oxygenated. Stretch out your arms, expand your ribcage and allow air to come in. When doing pranayama, think of the beautiful ancient

---

[4] The opening statement of Patanjali's *Yoga Sutras* is that this is a technique to still the wavering mind. Refers to calming the mind through the meditative techniques of Patanjali yoga.

statement 'Our source is completeness.' *Poornamidam.*
That is the state in which the mind expands from being an
ordinary limited mind, moving from 'I am only this' to 'I
am much more than this'.

*Q: Physical postures are what the world commonly labels as
yoga. Apart from physical fitness, what are its other benefits?*

Hatha yoga makes the body fit but yoga is not only physical.
It deals with the endocrine system too. It is also about the
psychological aspects. The physical is connected very closely
to the mind. Asanas are done in such a way as to bring about
changes in the hormonal system. You can alter your mood
with physical asanas. Have a healthy body and healthy mind.

Hatha yoga lays great emphasis on the physical body
and teaches one about how to attain well-being through
physical exercises and moderation in diet. The golden rule
is moderation. Asanas are designed to keep the body supple,
massage the internal organs, and keep the channels clear for
the uninterrupted flow of energy. Apart from maintaining
flexibility of joints and muscles, the endocrine system is
also addressed. Blockages in the energy channels and in
the organs lead to deterioration in health and disease. It is
important to keep your spine erect and supple when you
sit to do meditation, then everything will be well-balanced.

In yoga, our spine is the flute, and it is usually full of
muck. *Kriya* is one of the ways to clean it up. We can only

clean it up and wait. He will sing only when He wants to. We can only wait.

Connect physical to psychological and then to the spiritual. It is like a ladder. A mind that is not calm and quiet and tranquil cannot understand the Truth that the Upanishads speak of. When that happens, it is the point from which one takes off to higher levels of consciousness. That takes you into samadhi, which is an altered state of consciousness in which the mind expands.

There's a story about a lion cub that got lost in the forest and was brought up by sheep. He behaved like a sheep. One day a pride of lions came and saw this sheep-lion. A lioness came and asked, 'What are you doing?' He replied with a 'baa-baa'. She dragged him to a pond of clear water and made him look at his reflection. He saw himself clearly for the first time and he roared.

The great teaching of the Upanishads is that you are lions, you have strength. Look up at the horizon. Look how much one can move, one can expand. We have hypnotised ourselves to believe that we are tiny, we are small, we are merely human and that we are going to die. Instead, say to yourself, 'All my life I have hypnotised myself to believe that I am a sheep when I am actually a lion.' De-hypnotise yourself and say, '*Poornamidam*. Our source is completeness. I too must be a spark of that supreme energy.'

Breath of Life

Q: There is so much emphasis in yoga, and in pranayama, upon our breath, but breathing is something we do automatically from the instant we are born. Why do we need to study it?

Your entire life from birth to death is based upon breath, yet it is neglected. Learn how to breathe properly. For centuries, the ancient Indian rishis experimented with ways to breathe, and ways to manipulate the breath and the life force.

The rishis were spiritual scientists who explored the mind, emotions, and consciousness. Yoga is a science. It does not belong to any religion. The sages taught us about the link between breath and our emotions. They found that emotions can change the pattern of your breathing. Your mental state is reflected in your breath. When you are agitated, close your eyes and watch your breath, which moves very fast. They also discovered that if you change the rhythm and pattern of breathing, you can change your emotional state. Out of this came the science of pranayama.

Prana means life energy. The energy that goes into our system includes oxygen, which is also an energy, and other energies. The digestive fire is *prana*. *Prana* also helps us to excrete.

Yama means rules. Pranayama means rules and regulations of *prana*. It does not necessarily mean *swasa*, or breath. We cannot directly touch the *prana*. We can only connect to *prana* through our breath, which is intimately linked to that. If you can make your breath slow or fast, you can adjust your *prana* accordingly.

Yogic theory is that there are many *pranas* in the body, and *prana* operates through innumerable *nadis*, or channels, in the body. Three *nadis* are the most important, *Ida*, *Pingala*, and *Sushumna*. *Ida*, the left channel is associated with the moon and coolness. *Pingala*, the right one, is associated with the sun and fire. Moving up and down the spine in the *Sushumna nadi* is the main *prana*. In yogic terms, it is the movement of the aspiration for and concentration on either the higher or lower side. When it descends it leads to material well-being, and when it ascends it leads to spiritual well-being.

In yoga, one also understands that balancing the *Ida* and the *Pingala*, the left and right nostrils, keeps the lungs fully irrigated with air. When you manipulate the left nostril, *Ida* is working to full capacity. When you manipulate the right, *Pingala* is working to full capacity. Alternate between the two. In most people the *pranas* are unbalanced and not in proper symmetry.

Until now, your breath went on without your knowledge. Sit and watch your breath coming in and watch it going out. Balance your breath. Breath is also the link to the inner life.

Q: Can you tell us some simple, practical methods to do pranayama?

Hum-Sau breath meditation is a practical technique. First chant aloud 'Om' three times. Then give attention to your breath. Become aware of your breathing. Draw in a deep breath. As you breathe in, chant the sound of *hum*. When breathing out, chant the word *sau*. Give it your complete attention. Breathing in and breathing out is one single round. Practice about twenty rounds very slowly. Then stop saying the words and simply watch your breath carefully. Do that for some time. Then stop and bow down.

Most people do wrong breathing, surface breathing. Learn how to actually fill your lungs with air.

Anulombh vilombh, alternate nostril breathing, is where the *Ida* and the *Pingala*, left and right, are balanced. Sit comfortably with your spine erect. Close your right nostril. The traditional hand mudra is to fold in the forefinger and middle finger or hold your hand any way you choose. Close your right nostril. Take a slow deep breath through the left nostril. Then close the left nostril and breathe out from the right. Breathe in again from the right nostril. Exhale from the left. Don't bother counting, just do it as long as is comfortable. Five to ten minutes will do. Then sit quietly for a while. Allow your breath to settle down naturally.

Your lungs will be strengthened. You might feel a bit giddy the first time since your system is not used to receiving so much oxygen, and totally expelling carbon dioxide.

Q: Do you have any other tips?

There are innumerable pranayamas.

Bhastrika pranayama is one, and it is also known as bellows breathing.

Pot breathing or *Kumbhak* is another one. *Kumbhak* means pot. Take a deep breath. Push your breath all the way down to the stomach. Hold. Exhale. Do it for five minutes. Count if you wish to. Breathe in for ten counts. Hold for fifteen. Exhale for fifteen. Or use the count of ten–fifteen–ten. Don't allow the breath to rush out. And don't retain the breath for so long that you feel suffocated.

Deep breathing with both nostrils together is important. When outdoors in fresh air, in a garden or by the sea, take in a deep breath. Fill the upper chest fully. Stretch out your arms. Push the air down to the stomach. Then pull the stomach in and bring the air up again. Exhale. All this can be done in two seconds. Repeat. That helps to supply more oxygen to the lungs.

Kapalabhatti pranayama helps in cleaning the *kapala*, or head. Very helpful when coping with sinus congestion.

When your breath becomes rhythmic and silent, then your mind too becomes rhythmic and quiet. Everything

will fall silent within you, and you will not waste your
energy. There will be no distractions of the mind. Then
you can go deep within to search for your true identity.
You can go home to yourself.

The Split Mind

Q: The mind is capricious. It can flip over in an instant, flit all over the globe, and it can justify any action. How can one harness one's mind?

You create your own fiction of life. Vedanta teaches us that reality is not external to your mind. Instead, it is your mind that is reflected in matter. It is because of images that we have built up in our minds that we get hurt and we have problems. The world is real, but it is only relatively real. Not absolutely real. That means you don't actually know it. It may not be what you imagine it to be, or what you think it is. Quantum physics admits that two different observers would come to different conclusions about facts, and that reality is subjective. The observer is important.

The study of the mind is a very scientific one. We have the instruments to do that. The ancient sciences of Vedanta and yoga study the structure of the mind. The Bhagavad Gita is a classic text not only for managing the mind but also on how to study the mind.

Our minds also give colour to the past and the future. We create images for ourselves that become more important than the reality. We may not even know our own reality. And since it is not possible to conform to all these images, life becomes frustrating.

Modern life is full of distractions, both immediate and global. You could be doing one thing and thinking of something else. The mind is distracted out of habit, and that is one of our biggest problems. When you sit to meditate, distractions flood in. How do we stop being slaves of our minds? By awareness, both inner awareness and outer awareness. Watch the mind. Sit and watch your breath coming in and watch it going out. If you focus fully on that, everything will become quiet. The mind will stop racing and settle down.

Running away from one's circumstances is not the solution. Do internal vipassana, which means to see yourself clearly.

Q: We're told to keep an open mind. But doesn't that create confusion in our **minds and in our lives?**

Babaji told me, 'Don't put a full-stop anywhere. Don't think that you know everything.' I always bear that in mind.

One day I drove my red car to meet the Dzogchen Rinpoche at the Karnataka border, at Kollegal, on the way to Coimbatore. I arrived at a big Buddhist settlement, a monastery with a lot of agricultural land around it and met a thickset Tibetan who helped me park my car. Then he disappeared and I went in. A young Tibetan girl at the reception asked if I had an appointment with the

Rinpoche, but I did not. She went and returned to say the Rinpoche would meet me. She ushered me into a plush office and the same man who had helped me park my car outside was seated there. I looked round, but there was nobody else in the room. He was the Rinpoche. His opening line was 'I came out to welcome you'. I had taken a white silk scarf with me, he had one ready and we exchanged scarves. I asked to stay for a few days because I wanted to read a certain text. He asked a few questions about my background and if I was vegetarian, then told me to wait and went out. He returned with an English translation of *Kunzang Lama'i Shelung–Words of my Perfect Teacher*, written by an ancient teacher of the Ngima order. They gave me a room upstairs in the monastery to stay in and read the book. It touches upon all aspects of Tibetan Buddhism, including Dzogchen. Five days later, it was time for me to leave and I asked him where I could get a copy, whereupon he presented me with the book. I never met that man again. No need to meet again. I had got what I was looking for.

Such things are in the scheme of things. It is all part of the Happening. Even after my years with Babaji, and all that happened at the time, I still felt like I learnt something when I met that Rinpoche. Keep an open mind. There are many things you can learn from people.

I see the Boddhisattva's qualities in everybody, not only in one single person. They come in different forms, sometimes as benign deities, and sometimes as wrathful deities. But they are all deities. I am talking about an attitude that sees the divinity in everyone. When you meet a terrible man, just say to yourself, this is a manifestation of the wrathful deity, so that you don't begin to hate that person. I cannot live with hate and have thrown it out. When I was young, I had strong reactions and hated things, but there is no point in that. I rehearsed opening the window and throwing it out, many times, and finally got rid of it. I don't hate anybody now. Throw it out.

Q: With so much inner chatter in the mind, how is it possible to see the truth?

If you are serious about finding the truth, going beyond deceptions and appearances, then you must cease to grab or grasp. People tend to cling to things. Any pleasure of the senses will have some pain behind it. The greatest pain is to lose the pleasure we are enjoying.

Branding is built up to create desire. In day-to-day life it is not possible to be desireless. Some might want to become rich and famous, and the desire for security, companionship and affection is universal. Even to want to look good every day, to be neat and clean, that too is a desire.

You cannot leave the world and go elsewhere because your mind would still be caught up in the world. But if you go to the root of desire and crack it, then you will actually be free in the ultimate sense, as free as the breeze. Then a person could be driving an expensive car and not get caught in the sense of ownership.

It is possible to reach a point where you can transcend the desire for security, companionship and affection, but the difficulty is that people cannot let go. Some might say, 'I can live without such-and-such', but that's only an expression. They cannot give anything away. They feel everybody is conspiring to take away their money, and it makes them insecure. People fear that if they give away something, it will all go, they will be left with nothing and become poor.

When all grasping stops, when the mind is still, then you touch spirituality. Do it through constant practise. In the Vedas, Sadguru means the Brahman. It is the definition of the Supreme Being. The Supreme Being is the guru for everyone. If you truly believe that you can be led by the Supreme Being, then there is no distraction.

Then the silence will descend. In the silence, you will come to know your true self. Silence vibrates with Truth.

Everyone has to find their own solution. It means living and striving to improve, and to apply the principles afresh.

A yogi is not confined to old skeletons.

Q: What about the negativities of the mind? How does one cope with depression, anxiety, suffering and the daily sorrows that drip into our lives?

Suffering exists, we cannot escape it. Sorrow exists. We must accept that. We don't know why. We don't know why gravity exists. The ultimate 'why?' of many things is beyond the grasp of our limited minds. We have to accept it, and acceptance is the first step.

There is no creation without some suffering and stress. A child suffers in birth. The mother suffers in giving birth. These are facts.

Come face to face with it, don't avoid it. Cultivate an intimate friendship with it, then you will find that sorrow no longer remains sorrow.

It is all depends upon how you look at suffering. When great saints suffered, it was not like the suffering of others. Maharishi Ramana had cancer and there was pain but no suffering. He had nothing to do with the cancer. Ramakrishna Paramahansa too had cancer of the throat, was in pain, could not eat, but was in divine ecstasy. In the end you understand that you are not the sufferer. Then you are free. You must be mature enough to get to that point. But do not think that mysticism has to do with self-inflicted suffering. It's not a holy thing. Don't be violent towards yourself. Enjoy yourself. You will not be liberated and happy by deliberately inflicting suffering on your body.

Suffering and happiness are two sides of the same coin. The intervals in between suffering we call happiness. We want to hold on to that, but that doesn't happen either.

You cannot remove negativity by constantly thinking about it. You need to replace it with positive thinking. One of the aspects of the phrase 'let go and rejoice' is to mentally let go of it and live in the present moment.

Never do anything when you are angry because all your calculations may go wrong, so let your anger cool down before you act.

And while it is a good thing to cultivate positive thoughts and keep negative thoughts at bay, from the point of pure spiritual understanding, there is no positive or negative thought. Thought itself is a corruption. The freer you are from it, the better. The ultimate well-being is when the mind is quiet and calm and resting in the Supreme Being, whose very essence is happiness.

Q: *Is happiness the true nature of the mind? If so, why do we lose it so quickly?*

The true inner essence of every human being is joy. It is an ever-flowing stream of bliss. When you find it, you can relish all outer joys and happiness without grasping. The inner, settled state is the only sure route to joy. When you reach it, you will no longer search for it outside. Then you feel satisfied.

Sages for thousands of years have attained it and told us about it, and they cannot all be promoting a myth about peace, joy, stability, tranquillity. They attained it, and that opens up the possibility for all others.

When outer joy comes accept it but do not try to hold on to it, so when sorrow comes, as it will, it will not touch you. If you try and hold on to outer joy because it is rare, then enjoyment is lost because you become fearful of losing it.

Understand that the spark of the divine is in your heart, which is the essence of all happiness. To attain that, you need to have some control over your emotions, your thoughts, the way you view people and be free of obsessions of what happened yesterday.

Intelligent men and women will soon discover their own limitations, physically, emotionally, psychologically and spiritually. If you don't know where you stand, how will you take the next step to search for something else? It is not a mass movement. Today, people have evolved enough to live in this world and still attain spiritual heights.

On Home and Hearth

The House of Marriage

Q: What is the significance of marriage in the 21ˢᵗ century? The situation is slightly different in India and slightly different in the West, but marriage can be one of the biggest challenges in life.

Marriage is a challenge. Couples marry for their own reasons, not necessarily for a good life together. It's better if there is great mutual love, but even then there are problems and failures. But if that love is not even genuine, then the foundation is not strong.

There's no such thing as a perfect marriage. Much before getting married, or being in a relationship, we need to train our minds. Sri Ramakrishna Paramahansa put it simply: 'Before cutting and preparing the jackfruit, we apply oil so the hands won't become sticky'. That applies to everything.

If you want to get married, then enter the picture by understanding that you will need to make an adjustment. You may succeed, you may not, but there should be no heartburn at separation, no pain and sorrow. And if you get married, know that sometimes you may be right, and sometimes the other partner may be right.

In India, even today, many marriages are arranged, especially in villages. When arranged marriages largely prevailed, they were held in place by familial, cultural and social pressures. It could even be a family business arrangement. It was not good to break a marriage. Even if the couple did not love each other, they carried on, but those days are gone. Today, arranged marriages are not the norm, apart from village society.

Traditions are breaking down. For example, earlier, sannyasins[1] were Brahmins. That is not true today. So, *desh* and *vesh*, country and appearance, can all change.

Even when divinity descends upon earth as *Avatars,*[2] they have to change their appearance. They do so in order to live like other humans. But within, inside them, they are pure. I would say that one could live like that.

---

[1] A religious ascetic who renounces the world by performing his own or her own funeral and abandoning all claims to social or family standing.

[2] An embodied being considered to be God incarnate.

I am not a sannyasi. I too have a family, wife and children. For living in this world, we have to do all that needs to be done, but within us, we have to be neat and clean. This is possible. To demonstrate that, Babaji told me to go back to the world and live the life of a householder. He said, 'Do so because the people who come to you will be mostly householders. If you shave your head and become a sannyasi, what will you be able to tell them? Then what you would know would be second-hand knowledge.'

Q: Marriage can be an arena of conflict instead of harmony. How to cope?

Part of that came with the unconscious belief that the man is superior to the woman.

People are thinking freely now. Each one has their own thought processes. If a couple love each other, that love could endure, but there are difficulties too and only those who are intimate would know that.

Nowadays, if a man or woman do not want to live with the partner, married or not, they can get out. People follow the easy route, which leads to break-ups and divorce. They think, 'This won't work now so I must get out of it.' In some religions, marrying and divorcing is not so difficult, but in some cultures, divorce is still considered wrong.

So, the members of this new generation, faced with this confusion, do not favour these institutions. They do not have the time to study all this. When we have domestic problems, we can decide things only after examining things deeply. The main reasons for problems are that people are self-centred, and any foreign body is soon expelled.

The only way out is to transform the mind to goodness. Any external reformation won't help here. It will not work.

Q: Isn't marriage considered to be a building block of a stable society?

We can't be assured that marriage is the building block of society. We can't be sure of that anymore. We are in a new era. Today the significance of marriage has reduced.

Human beings, when they developed society, discovered that there are certain benefits to marriage, and the institution was constituted. But traditions are breaking down, and the institution of marriage has lost some of its importance. You can patch it up, but it may not be the same ever again.

The institution of family too has changed. Family structures are different. Joint families are no longer the same. The new generation wants to live on their own. They think differently.

Q: The other aspect is loneliness if one is unmarried. That is particularly so in the West, where the extended family structure is very different from India. Children grow up and leave home. What about loneliness?

Children get busy and caught up in looking after themselves. They don't have time to take care of their parents or talk to them. It's not a lack of affection.

Loneliness of parents left behind is a problem that has to be solved. We have to create a new dimension in modern society. We need more people to give voluntary care.

If you don't want to get married, you can have good companions, good friends.

Who Is a Woman?

Q: It's been a man's world for many centuries. Most women have big or little problems of low self-worth and self-esteem. What do you feel is the position of women today?

Women have something special in them. Debunk all the myths you may have heard that women belong to some lesser category, are always dependent and have to be supported. They have an extraordinary role to play in society because they are different. Men must accept that.

Women too have to change their own mindset. They must understand that if they come from a culture that deems them to be inferior then they must change that, and they can change it. Women have to be helped to get self-esteem. Otherwise, we are controlling their freedom. We cannot adjust to a chauvinistic society.

Society became male-oriented, historically. We must change that, and change can be painful. Anything worthwhile can happen only when some structures are broken down, and new ones come up.

We have had several male *Avatars* and now the next one needs to be female. I am not talking about women gurus but an *Avatar*. It is time that the Universal Mother incarnates herself on this earth and sets right the imbalance that continues to exist.

Adi Shankaracharya, who came from an orthodox background, after writing his commentaries on the

Vedas and Upanishads, wrote the beautiful *Soundarya Lahiri*. In that delightful chant he extols the beauty of the Devi in no uncertain terms. The title means 'the ecstasy of beauty'.

Q: Today we live in knowledge economies. Earlier, brute strength ruled the world and women could not compete, but today a woman can be as highly educated and as mentally powerful as a man. What is the way forward?

Women's empowerment is a term commonly used today. What I refer to as empowerment is bringing women into all domains of work that men do. How do we bring women into the public domain? Through education and self-confidence.

Women must have the capacity to sit face to face with anyone and talk courageously. We must give them that courage. This freedom and courage must be given in childhood by parents and by schoolteachers. If they have this training, they will find the rest for themselves.

Q: Domestic abuse and violence against women is prevalent in all countries and in all classes of societies. Paedophile gangs also operate everywhere. These are big issues. What about India?

That should be easier to counter in India where the female Shakti, the dynamic cosmic energy, has been worshipped, and every woman is a potential Kali. But women have not been well-treated here, and Swami Vivekananda said many of the difficulties faced by India is because women have not been well-treated.

A woman is also a mother. A mother carries a baby in her womb for ten months, and that establishes a link that a man, the father, does not have. She nurtures and protects the child, and that comes naturally to a mother. After that, it is unacceptable for a man to mistreat women when a woman has placed him here on earth. Whosoever ill-treats a woman will reap the karmic consequences. Nobody gets away with anything spiritually, not even the smallest action.

Mother Earth also sustains us so compassionately, even though our actions wreak havoc on her day in and day out, polluting her sacred breath.

The *Shaktas*[3] are called *Shaktas* because they believe the divine form is most evidently manifest in woman. How then can a woman be considered not sacred?

Woman is Shakti, the creator.

Each woman is a Shakti.

Just realize it.

---

[3] *Shaktas* are the worshippers of the goddess, called Shakti or Devi, in India.

Q: Is the difference between men and women only physical? What are the advantages and disadvantages of being a woman?

The difference between men and women is not just physical, because of the different body shape, but also a difference in sensations and feelings. Different psychological make-up, different movements of inner feelings. The flip side is that a woman can be so emotional that she may not be able to easily get hold of these emotions, which a man could do more readily.

There are also some external compulsions. If a man wants to leave home, it is easier for him, even today. If a woman becomes homeless there are other risks. So, women should learn self-defence and martial arts. If women are abused, they should fight back, then they will not be touched again.

About Children

Q: How does one raise children to become sensible adults?
Marriage also provides a context for children, with role
models in both parents.

After all our duties and responsibilities in life have been
carried out, our children will take them forward. We
must all work in return for using the resources of this
earth.

Children need to learn to search for happiness,
freedom and inner strength. To learn to live free. We
have reached a stage where we don't need to carry
information in our heads. Technology can help us move
out of that space, and information is available at the
touch of a fingertip.

A proper understanding is more important than
information gathering. We think problems can only
be solved through intellect, but many things can be
solved when you are down-to-earth. It is important to
observe and understand the world around us, then we
gain perspective. Children observe and learn from their
surroundings, but as we grow up we sometimes stop
paying attention to the world around us. Some may hold
the best degrees but have not really met human beings
face to face. Only by living in the world can you say you
have truly matured. If we do not go through difficulties,

do not one understand the problem, then how can we solve it?

Children have to be brought up in an environment of free thinking and proper understanding. I like folk songs because nobody tells you that this music is right and that is wrong. They just throw themselves into it and what comes out is music.

Evolution has followed a certain pattern for millennia, but now we have to change that. Now is the opportunity to open up different parts of our brain. Ask, 'can we open up, make our minds blossom?' Education should include that. We are in the next evolutionary scale.

There are many bright sparks I see out there, and I hope they will become a big fire.

Q: What is truly a good education for children? They can feel burdened with too much work, and schools can be very expensive, thus creating a burden for parents.

Education has become linear. In daily life you have a job and have to use your logical mind. Instead of competing with others, try to excel at what you do.

In childhood now we are too exposed to TV, internet, social media, advertising, and our minds become scattered. By the time a child grows up, the mind is already confused and disturbed.

There are many different ways of understanding things. Intellect has somehow become associated with Western intellectualism, but the Upanishadic way of looking at things is different. Earlier, the young child would have become a *Brahmachari*, a celibate student, and the mind would become disciplined and have the time to mature. Children were given moral precepts and then encouraged to get on with their lives.

Education is also about getting to know yourself, quite apart from having the tools to earn a living. It is about learning how to conduct yourself well, and learning about inner capacities, which are not explored. Some people unconsciously manifest a few, but we need to have mastery over our minds. Instead, our minds have mastery over our lives, often with destructive results through negative emotion and thought. We need to observe our own mental processes, to inculcate the discipline and training to study the nature of the mind. Schools do not emphasize this training of the mind. If this training is imparted in childhood, that would make it easier to enter into harmonious relationships in the world.

We have reached the maximum of material development. Now understand that nothing can be supported from the outside, it has to be supported from the inside out.

To Love

Q: Love is a loaded word, and it comes with both good baggage and rotten baggage. Religion proclaims it, but just look at the violence and the bloody wars fought in its name. How can one define love, understand it?

Love is not a moral law for discussion, but a deliberate practise in life. If you practise affection and drop hate, you will notice the difference in those around you. Be pure of heart. Let us purify our hearts and have no hatred for anyone. Then there is only love. Then there would be heaven on earth.

Love and hate are two sides of the same coin. It just depends upon your point of view. There may be someone you have hated for years. Ask yourself, 'Can I change that? How can I change to make that person happy?' That thought will impact your heart and physical well-being too. I speak from experience. There was someone I hated when I was about nineteen. Babaji told me to meditate and visualize that person in front of me and offer him flowers. It was very hard at first. But after some days, that person's image disappeared.

My heart is clean. I don't hate anyone. I practised putting hate in a black rubbish bin bag every night and flinging it out of the window. Don't carry your anger, hatred and poisonous feelings over from one day to the next. Wake up fresh in the morning and say to yourself, 'Yesterday is gone. Can I be fresh today?'

Love, affection, compassion must be practised and experienced. They are not to remain concepts hidden in dusty tomes. Talking about it won't do at all. We speak of other religions and other nations, but when you don't hate anyone, love prospers. I am reminded of what the Bible says, 'Blessed are the pure in heart, for they shall see God'.

Q: How can we make a reality of love in life? How can we truly practise it? How does one expand one's consciousness? Is love the same as compassion?

Compassion is a big word and not always easy to connect with. 'Love' is more understandable. When you see your neighbour suffering and want to alleviate his suffering, that is love. Be kind. Be humane. Conduct yourself in such a way that wherever you go, whatever you do, people will remember you with admiration.

It is impossible to avoid having likes and dislikes, except for very few, but at least do not harbour hatred in your heart.

One might have to be stern to discipline someone at times, but that too needs to be done with love and not hate. When people who meet me are scolded, they don't feel bad because they know they have been scolded out of love.

People have a strange idea about love if they say they love Krishna or Jesus, or someone else, but are callous and cruel towards other human beings. Instead of proclaiming your love for some exalted star outside, first look at yourself. Are you self-centred? Do you care for others? It is not possible to be on the spiritual path without caring for others.

Q: How can you speak about love to the agents of violence and hatred? Terrorists and others who murder and plunder.

Approach it with the attitude that perhaps you can go in and clean up some of the mess. Ahimsa (non-violence) is not a moral practice but a practical technique. It is an action to calm one's mind.

I spent time with Naxalites and other groups holding extreme views. I talked to them over a cup of tea. I didn't give them anything except a compassionate hearing and as much dignity as I would give any human being.

They said, 'I was in hiding. My clothes are torn, I haven't had a bath.' I replied, 'It doesn't matter. I can smell you. Why are you suffering and causing others to suffer?' None of them want their children to become like them, which means they don't like themselves. You can only reform people when they question themselves. They felt the world is not treating them well, that all governments are imperialistic. But they also saw how selfish their own group was, and how badly they treated even their own people. If you appreciate people, they become better. Sometimes it worked and they gave up their violent practices, but not always.

That happened because my mind has settled down, because I have established tranquillity in the inner self, and they began to experience it too. For the past year there have been no murders in that district.

Become more human, more kind to others. Society is made up of individuals. The change in one individual will be mirrored in the human collective consciousness. Love and hatred have equal potential to spread.

Q: Is love desire? Is it lust? They say love is blind, and couples in love cannot see anything else.

The most transparent love is when two people are so in love with each other that they are ready to jump into fire if need be but won't be parted from each other. That is also biological.

Is love desire? If so, it leads to fear, jealousy, division and the aggressiveness to possess, to become something. Love should not be qualified with sentimentality, which is erratic and ever-changing.

Instead of *falling* in love, why not rise up in love?

Heart Matters

Q: The heart seems to be beyond our ken. Hearts get broken, are given away in love, dance with joy, jump into the mouth with fear, hearts speak to us, and we can become heartsick with grief. Sometimes hearts even fail. So, what is it?

How do we define the heart? The Upanishads declare it is that which cannot be described in words. It is not a physical entity. It is the core of one's consciousness. Of course, there is the physical heart that pumps blood.

The undefinable characteristics of the heart go back to ancient teachings. When you clean-up the commanding self that keeps dictating to you then what remains is the heart. It comes with love. You cannot invoke it through intellectual means or scholarship. It happens when someone purely loves. The ultimate love of merging with the Supreme is one thing. But even ordinary love, like when you walk down the street and see a little child crying, and you pick up the child and hold it close to your heart, even there the real heart begins to function. If that heart-full-ness is not there, if you don't reach that, then all our theories, all our teachings are of no use.

We must ask ourselves, 'Who am I?'

My master Maheshwarnath Babaji used to say, 'When you take off your shoes, leave your ego also there and come in. When we approach sacred spots, we remove our shoes before going in.'

When Moses walked up the mountain, he took off his shoes because he was stepping on sacred ground. And what did he see? A burning bush. There was a light behind the bush. Moses asked the question which is important for all of us, 'Who are you?' The answer was, 'I am That I am.' or 'I will Be what I will Be.' Thus encompassing the past, present and future.

When a human being purifies himself through love and through discipline, then the heart opens up. You begin to have an understanding of the unfathomable Something that is full of bliss.

On the World and You in It

The Clout of Power, Wealth, Sex

Q: Power, wealth and sex seem to be the three major energies in the world, and they can be overwhelming. How does one understand them, put them into some perspective and not lose one's balance?

Money can buy power, and power can help achieve wealth. What do people worship? Wealth? Fame? Power? Pleasure? Then follow pride, lust, the envy of others, and you've often heard it said that power corrupts.

Nobody can say, 'I have absolute power.' That's not possible as long as one exists in the physical body and identifies oneself with the limited self.

But one could say, 'I have touched some deep channels that link me to the Absolute Power.' That power opens up the vast mind inside us, and it also lies beyond the mind. Then the mind in its depths is liberated because it is free of attachment. You feel lighter and feel relieved. Otherwise, you narrow down your mind and thoughts.

Understand that at some point all worldly activity will cease. In the Upanishad, Agni, the God of fire, is considered to be a powerful deity. Agni has the capacity to burn and equalise. Fire is a symbol of the spirit. Fire had to be made in ancient times by rubbing dry flint, and fire came from a spark. There's also an inner spark in us. That inner Self manifests itself for a span of years, and then returns back to the unmanifest.

Q: Sex is used in advertising to sell everything from ice cream to soap. It is also a fast route to fame and fortune. How does one resist such allure?

Sex is only entertainment. The sex instinct is in-built by nature. Money came later. Power is used to obtain the other two. Consider sex like the food you eat or anything else. That it's something natural – you can do it and then leave it there. If you don't get obsessed, then it loosens its grip. The desire will fall away altogether when you discover other enjoyment within you that is well beyond anything sexual.

A yogi wants to gain spiritual power and enjoy bliss, but he doesn't need trinkets. The awakening of the kundalini in us, the Serpent Power, the spiritual orgasm, is far more blissful than sex.

Too much stress has been laid on celibacy, so much so that one is then obsessed with that idea. When you are obsessed with something, you end up thinking about that constantly. Your mind has a way of working on what you're thinking about. Then it goes to the senses. Your mind has a way of attracting that very same thing you wish to avoid or fear, and it comes to you, and keeps coming back.

It also causes sexual aberrations. Why not just let it be and carry on with your life? Why give it special importance? Many other things are more important.

Q: In this day and age, don't you think proper **sannyasa**,[1] *not only physical but mental and emotional as well, is very difficult? Is it even possible?*

In this day and age, full *sannyasa* is difficult. Mentally it is difficult, but possible. Emotionally, also possible. *Sannyasa* doesn't mean you become a zombie with no emotions, but it means the emotions are refined.

To actually take full *sannyasa* means to live solely on alms. A sannyasi is not supposed to have an organisation, or relationships and attachments. Also, *sannyasa* is associated with complete celibacy. How many people can do that?

---

[1] Sannyasa is renunciation. It includes renunciation of sex and leading a life of sexual chastity.

People who take vows of absolute celibacy may not always succeed.

Why not NOT be a sannyasi?

I do not feel this is the age when people need to become renunciates. It is not necessary to be celibate, instead you can live a simple life, and not get caught up in the trappings.

Money's Worth

Q: Money is a major energy in the world, but what is its actual meaning for us?

Don't take the vow of poverty. The new spiritual evolution is not sworn to poverty. That's not real. In the modern world, we cannot go back to the days of renunciation.

Take the vow of plenty. No need to reject anything, but at the same time try to truly grasp the impermanence of life. While increasing your riches, increase your inner life too. Find the balance.

There's no need to abandon anything. Money is a major energy in the world. Just give up exclusivity. Have. Share. Give. The world belongs to ALL. Life evolved by sharing. Humans evolved from chimpanzees by cooperating, sharing, working together. Young people, if they understand and embrace this, can invent a wonderful future.

We create problems for ourselves because of our obsession with money. Wealth can be like cancer, which overtakes the entire system because some cells have simply forgotten to stop multiplying. We can also forget to stop multiplying wealth. Thus, we can clog the drain.

Money represents a desire for fulfilment. It brings comfort and opportunities, but can that give total fulfilment, or is there something else as well? Wealth can also create a lack of ease, and can bring conflict, pain and sorrow. Nobody knows when death will come and take it all away.

Q: Why do people find it difficult to part with money and other possessions?

We need to have a spiritual understanding of money from the point of view of the soul. Giving is important and we do it for ourselves. For our own satisfaction. For our own happiness. For the feel-good factor in us. And there, attitude is more important than meditation. Learn that, and live happily in the world.

You can only share what you have. That includes spiritual wealth and material wealth. You cannot give away what you don't possess. Renunciation rings hollow if you do not have anything in the first place to give away.

Learn how to handle wealth, how to use it wisely, not misuse it. The stress in our lives lies in our busyness and always looking to accumulate more and more. We will have a sense of relief when we unload the busyness of the mind. The rich and the poor both have to sleep, and both have to die. Know that all these things given to you will be left behind.

There is a story about Guru Nanak and the needle. The great guru travelled widely, teaching people to work hard and be generous, opening free *langars* (kitchens) offering food to all. A merchant held a feast in the guru's honour. Dhuni Chand was very wealthy, and very miserly.

After the feast, Guru Nanak gave him a needle, saying, 'You are a careful man. Please take this needle. After I die, we will meet in the next world, then you can return the needle to me.' Dhuni Chand became anxious. 'How am I going to carry this needle in death and give it back to you?' Guru Nanak replied that if he could not even carry one needle with him into the afterlife, how did he suppose he would take his gold, palaces, elephants and servants with him? That taught Dhuni Chand the valuable lesson that he could take nothing with him when he died, so why not use it now to help those who needed it? Even if you live in a golden palace, know that you cannot take it with you when you die.

The Hunt for Happiness

Q: Why is there so much misery in the world? Even those who have all material comforts are still not satisfied. What is the nature of happiness? And why does it elude so many people?

Everyone seeks to be happy. Who does not want that? We collect many things and want more and more gratification. People go on holiday, take drugs and drink, but when the experience has passed, they are back to square one. That's because the whole search lies in temporary objects and experiences.

Your mind is telling you that you are incomplete, but that is not true. Your mind goads you into the endless pursuit of happiness. Everyone has his or her own subjective idea of happiness. A child wants toys, ice cream, TV cartoons and suchlike. When we grow up, we want different things. How much money do we have in the bank? Will we be able to continue to live in the same luxury? As we change and become middle-aged and older, our concept of happiness too changes.

Q: We look at images of rich and famous people and envy their happiness. We want to be like that. Is that happiness?

We are preoccupied all the time with 'becoming somebody' in the world. The search for happiness pushes us on, but where will you finally find it? If you feel you find happiness in this or that, wealth or fame, then why do you continue to constantly search for it after you get that? The answer is obvious. All our lives, we search for happiness in material things, thinking that the key is a big bank balance, a palatial house, a beautiful wife or something else, but we never really find it. We don't find happiness because we are never satisfied with anything that we have.

We may feel satisfied for a while after possessing the object of our desire, but in the long run we keep on searching. That even leads us to the desperate point where we just want to grab it and run. The truth is that the happiness we keep on seeking evades us. It seems slippery, staying just out of reach. The moment we get hold of one bit of happiness we try to hold on to it for dear life. Somehow, somewhere, we feel that it is so rare that it can vanish.

If you hold on to something and, simultaneously, if there is a fear at the back of your mind about losing it, where is the happiness now? There is only insecurity. Can you ever be happy when you are insecure and fear losing it? That is not happiness. So, the endless search continues with flitting from one thing to the other. The search takes us to many things. If you are single, you think you will be happy if you get married. Or you think you will be happier if you have some more money. You might feel the height of happiness is to own a Rolls Royce. Human beings have always been searching for happiness.

Q: Does that mean one must turn one's back on the pleasures of life?

I am not saying we should not enjoy the little joys to be found in day-to-day life. Please do enjoy the greatest and most wonderful things the world has to offer us. The morning dewdrop, the breeze that gently wafts to us the scent of jasmine, the fragrance of the earth after the first monsoon rain, the snowy peaks of distant mountains, the laughter of a child, a cup of tea. These are the little joys of life, but the lasting happiness we seek is not to be found outside oneself, in things material.

Q: If happiness has to be found independent of external objects, what is that source we need to tap?

We forget to look for happiness within. What you seek already exists inside you, it is already present. The seers suggest in the Upanishads and the Vedas, the great scriptures of India, that happiness can be independent of all external things. The Isavasya Upanishad tells us, 'Know that you are whole and complete in yourself. Recognize it and be happy.'

When there is that inner space, we find everything is within us. The wounds, hurts and hatred that we carry in our hearts is the biggest barrier to inner space. If you don't clean up this muck, there is no space for anything to happen.

Once having experienced this happiness, life becomes joyful. Then, every little thing is full of joy. All that was previously unnoticed, everything, becomes a festival of joy, and the root of this lies within oneself. When the inner being is happy, the world becomes full of joy for you.

The Sanskrit word for completeness is *poorna*. Fullness. Fulfilment. The Upanishads teach us that being complete, *poorna*, is the essence of our being. The Atman, the pure consciousness within each one, is complete and free of distractions. This is not exclusive to yogis. Everyone has it, but they do not know it yet. The way to find it is through sadhana (spiritual practices), which can be taught. If you long for something, no matter what you wish for, you will find a way to get it.

The student goes deep within his self under the guidance of the teacher. Then you realise your very nature is happiness. It is not something to search for outside.

Q: Is there a way to attain a settled state of happiness, remain fully satisfied and yet continue to live in this world and do the right thing?

Living in the world, experiencing life and embracing it, is the philosopher's stone which can eventually purify you and transform you from base metal into gold. Don't run away from the battle, instead stay and fight it out with love, affection and understanding.

The famous verse from Isavasya Upanishad is, '*Om poornamadah, poornamidam poornamudacyate, poornasya poornamadaya poornamevavasisyate.*'

Just as the outer world is full of divine consciousness, your inner world is full of the same divine consciousness.

That is not a riddle. It is a fact. You are a microcosm of the macrocosm. What does that mean? That means the divine consciousness that manifests itself in the universe is also the same substance that is within you. Search for what is already in you, realize it and be happy.

A genuine, realized yogi feels complete, and there are no desires left, no need for anything else. He is always happy.

The sages who experienced this joy went on to say 'That' happiness is an ecstasy, which is beautiful and all-embracing, and one feels like sharing it with all of humanity.

On Friendship

Q: What is the role of friends in life? We choose our friends, spend a lot of time with them, and may be more in tune with them than family.

People seek friendship at the click of a button on social networks, but who is there at the other end? You need the warmth of a human friend. The mind yearns for a friend who will respond to you. Learn to interact with people. Seek pure friendship. A friend brings joy to his or her friend and is helpful in times of trouble.

Relationships matter on the path of life. Spirituality connects hearts and all humanity together. It is a natural process. That is where a guru plays a role. Study the lives of saints. They lived for others, not for themselves. They created a happy atmosphere around them, were friendly with all, gave joy, freed others from pain. That is why they continue to live on in people's hearts. Walk with the guru, join your steps with his on the path and turn to divinity.

Q: What if a friend betrays you? That can be the unkindest cut of all.

People are looking after themselves. Friendship can be beautiful but human beings change. Don't be dependent on your friends, keep the reality of impermanence in mind. Live with friends but don't get caught up in a narrow circuit.

Do not find fault in others. We must introspect, and only then can we see the true picture.

Q: Are friendships with fellow spiritual pilgrims more trustworthy? And what of friendship with spiritual guides?

Spirituality does not create bondage but shows the divine dimension in relationships.

You must long for that grace above all else, seek it above all else. Converse constantly with the divine. Think of the jewel within. For that, an individual relationship with the teacher related to spiritual aspiration, not material existence, helps the seeker who yearns for grace. But if you fail in the path of practices, then you fail to develop the proximity to the teacher. That does not mean the inseparable relationship between teacher and disciple has ended, it merely means the student's quest for spirituality is not strong enough.

You may think spirituality is the solution to all your problems, but for that your thirst for spirituality needs to be very deep and strong. You also need a lot of patience. That patience will strengthen the bond with the teacher, and a strong bond can smoothen the path of spirituality.

Q: When friends get together, they gossip. In groups, in offices, on phones, on the net, people are chattering and gossiping all the time. What's your view?

Gossip is in the nature of human beings. Before the jet age and internet, gossip was the way in which news spread.

There can be good gossip, but gossip is only too often malicious and judgemental. Society becomes judgemental. In the West, people have more individual freedom, but the other side of that coin is loneliness. People can be very lonely, and that becomes a mental health issue.

Perhaps we should have a club for good gossip.

Feasting and Fasting

Q: People like to gather for feasts, to eat and drink and make merry. In India, there is a festival every day if one chooses to celebrate it. What's the importance of feasts and festivals?

Let every day be a fiesta. Enjoy looking at the parrot in the tree, the eagle sketching circles in the sky, the flowers in the gardens, the tastes, the sounds, the sights.

That is the feast of life but nobody is looking.

We create artificial feasts to entertain ourselves. Nothing wrong with that, as long as it doesn't deplete your health. The ancient Manu Dharma Shastra gives a good description of how an ideal householder should live. After completing the morning activities, he should meditate on the divine and then cook his food. After cooking, dedicate it to God. Then he should go his gate and ask three times, 'Is anyone hungry out there?' If there is a response, he should feed them first and only then eat himself.

To feed a hungry person is equal to ten days of *tapasya* (austerities).

Even if you don't do sadhana, giving will purify you. The outer works on the inner being, and the inner manifests in one's outer nature.

Awareness is also how you behave in this world, how you interact with others. It could be very simple. One day I found a child in rags crying on the pavement. Should I

79

risk picking him up, I wondered. I did pick him up. The mother rushed out from somewhere, and I took them both for a meal. The purest form of love is that of a mother for her baby.

Q: There seem to be an equal number of reasons to fast as to feast, especially in India. Is fasting recommended?

Occasional fasting is good for health and well-being. But prolonged fasts over several days and weeks should be avoided. They weaken the mind, and that's when others can take control of your mind. The insecurities of a person, the need to belong somewhere, is exploited by power-hungry people who begin to control your mind and create a hypnotic state. A great deal of violence occurs during those days, violence against 'the other'.

Violence will persist until we evolve further, and the time is approaching when that could happen. We should be aware of that, and actively participate to hasten the process. Struggle for that. Struggle is good. Even a handful of people who change can influence large numbers. Otherwise, we will dig the hole deeper, and it will be difficult to come out.

Giving Gifts

Q: You have said that you don't like to accept gifts. What is the reason?

Behind every gift there will be an attitude, or reason. Very few people give something out of sheer generosity and goodwill. Many people give gifts not because they are philanthropic but because of an ulterior motive. Let us say they go to a place of worship and make an offering of a big sum, which might make them feel that the offence or crime they have committed will be covered up. The intention matters, the motivation matters.

Non-acceptance of gifts is one of the *Yama* and *Niyama* in Patanjali's *Yoga Sutras*. There are many reasons for that, especially for yogis. The primary psychic reason is that when somebody gifts a yogi something, that gift carries with it the karmic effects of that person's life. At least part of it is transferred to him in some way, and they may have it in mind that the yogi will take away their pain and sorrow.

If you are a yogi, there are two parts to it. Either you feel you can accept the gift and stall the effects, or you are so sensitive that it may affect you, the vibration could affect you anyway. That is one of the karmic reasons. A genuine yogi will be able to handle it, but if someone is not a true yogi, then it is difficult to handle. *Yama* and *Niyama* are prescribed for yogis, and for those practising yoga.

The other reason is that I am here as a teacher. If somebody comes and gives a teacher a large sum of money, and if that teacher is not a completely free person, what happens next? He or she may begin to expect it. And then, if it is not offered again, he could get disappointed, even if he does not show it. The other part to this is that the person who does not come with a gift does not get as much attention if the teacher's mind is still caught up with the material world.

There are two people involved in gifts, not just one. The one who gives, and the one who receives. The person who receives must make sure his affection for that person is not dependent upon the gift.

Q: What about the gift of energy? An exchange of energy takes place between people when they meet. Does a yogi give a gift by touch?

Touching feet is an old tradition in India. In the case of a true yogi, the energy goes not only from the bottom to the top, but also from top to bottom. It's a cycle. Therefore, the belief is that if you touch the feet then the blessings of the yogi's energy will flow to you. That is the basis of that practice. It is not even a show of respect, but the possibility that you are partaking of the blessings of that person.

Also, by bowing down what you are really saying is, 'Look I am humble, I am surrendering to you, please help me.' For a really sensitive yogi that is fraught with danger. A lot of people bring their entire burdens and leave them at his feet when they touch them. Mentally, that's how they conceive of it. Then two things could happen. Either the yogi deliberately does not take up the burden but leaves it there, but that's not possible all the time.

The yogi's body and mind are sensitive and subtle, he has become very sensitive, and some of that illness and karmic burden might get transferred.

It is better if you do not physically touch a yogi or spiritual teacher.

Babaji generally did not allow anyone to touch his feet, but at times he permitted it. After a class on Upanishads, I would bow down. One day, I felt like touching his feet, but he said, 'Give me a hug.'

While there are rules, there are also times when one has to break the rules, depending upon your understanding and intelligence. One old lady came to see me, she had nothing to take, nothing to give. With the support of two persons, she was trying to bend down to touch my feet, but it would have been very difficult for her to get up again. What should I do? I was seated under the peepul tree and decided to raise my feet instead of letting her bend down, which could be misinterpreted as arrogance, but it made her happy. I discourage people from touching my feet. But there are exceptions when some good could be done to the other person.

The law was made for man, not man for the law.

Q: Does that mean one, and especially you, can never accept a gift without wondering? Surely all of life is an exchange.

No, that does not mean you should never accept a gift. My problem is that if I don't accept their gifts those persons might think they have done something wrong, or it would bring them bad luck if I do not accept it. It's a tight corner I am in.

We have to use our common sense. There is no harm if someone brings a flower to express love and affection.

Non-acceptance of gifts is meant especially for sadhus, sannyasins, in the *Yoga Sutras*. A sannyasin who is dependent on gifts it not free but has got stuck. He's not going anywhere. The yogi who is seeking *Kaivalya*, moksha or liberation, does not want to get caught up in that and has to be alert. He must be conscious of it at all times.

On Attitude

Look in the Mirror

Q: 'Know thyself.' We've heard this maxim for centuries, but how can people know themselves beyond, and apart from, the self-image of being a woman, or a man, black, white, rich, poor and all the other identities we have?

You look in the mirror but don't really see yourself as you are.

My master, Maheshwarnath Babaji, told me, 'Ask yourself: where do I stand? What is the position that I start from?' The first step is to understand yourself.

The way to study yourself, to 'self-realize', to see yourself as you are and not as you imagine you are, is to be part of society. When you get on a bus, and someone steps on your toes, then watch your own reaction. See who you really are. Do you get angry? Do you verbally, or silently, abuse him or her? The real content of your mind will become apparent.

When we are alone, there is nobody to interact with, to get angry with. We cannot get angry at the walls of our cave. You may feel that isolation is necessary for self-enquiry, but you cannot really understand yourself sitting alone. Come out of your cave.

Try and see yourself clearly without prejudice, judgment and without condemning yourself or too much self-criticism. Unless you recognize the intensity of the problem how will you be able to solve it?

Do not begin with the idea, 'I am great, I am blissful, I am this, or I am that.' Don't be distracted by such thoughts. Communicate and interact with others. Understand your strengths and your weaknesses. A great deal of attention is needed for this self-examination, and this is possible only in the midst of people.

Q: People can be very deceptive and cruel. What if somebody has been badly hurt, abused and exploited? What is the lesson there?

It is no use finding fault with others. The other person who is hurting you is actually getting hurt himself, but he doesn't realize that. Retribution will come to him, or her, not you. Never hate that person. Know that they are behaving badly out of ignorance. If you are on the spiritual path, then pray for that person. No need to interact with them but wish them well as they lead their own lives.

We have to look at ourselves. Only then do we see our true being within. Don't cling to hurts, hatreds and wounds and keep on fretting. Don't live in the past. Let go. Clean up the muck, throw it out, create space for the new. Allow good things to come in. Allow yourself the peace to go within.

Recognize the jewel inside you, which is inside everyone. It's a spark that is related to the omnipotent divinity within us, the light of which has the energy to clear all filth in us.

The question to ask yourself is, 'Who am I?'

That which we seek, whichever way we are travelling to it, is something intimate. We are actually searching for ourselves in our true essence. For that, you require a clear mind, not prejudiced by all that one has gathered. Without that, one can still have some spiritual experiences but may not reach the goal.

One of the functions of a spiritual teacher is to clean the mirror and hold it up to you. Even that has to be done very slowly, in a gentle way, so that people do not feel hurt. Nobody likes to see themselves in the mirror as they truly are. Nobody likes that. Either they will break the mirror or else they will run away. But if you don't see yourself clearly in the mirror, how will you ever change?

Q: There are many existential crises and bewildering choices to make in modern life, the pandemic being an extreme and recent example. Is there a formula for leading a fulfilling life?

It is no use running away from life. The four stages of life were clearly chalked out in ancient Hindu texts in order to realize the full human potential through knowledge, pleasure, wealth and wisdom leading to moksha, liberation. Nothing was excluded. It is sensible and very practical.

First, life as a student, *brahmacharya*.

Then the phase of marriage and raising children, or *grihastha* ashrama.

Then comes retirement, *vanaprastha* ashrama, after the children are married.

The final stage is *sannyasa*, a renunciate's life, when you prepare for inevitable death.

Thus, you would have completed all your responsibilities and feel fulfilled with your life on earth. The better path is to live a normal life.

It Must Touch Your Life

Q: How can one reconcile spiritual aspirations with the realities of earning money and managing practical affairs? Daily life in the world is challenging.

It is not something 'out there'. It is not far away. It is inside you.

Just bring it into your daily life. You must measure yourself in the world, and that is your touchstone to spiritual practice. By having a singular understanding of life and spirit you limit yourself and block a proper understanding of yourself and the universe.

Human beings who live almost entirely in the third dimension don't like change because it upsets their habits and routines. Get out of your comfort zone.

Women who have lived with support all their lives become dependent and find it difficult to have courage.

Q: Does one have to retire into solitude in order to connect with one's own spirituality?

Isolation makes you limited. The world around you is the arena of your spiritual practice. Intervals of solitude are necessary, but you cannot shut yourself off totally.

I got a divine call when I was nine and became absorbed in deep meditation. At nineteen, I was pulled towards the

Himalayas and quit my comfort zone to go and search for my guru.

My guru did not want me to drown in books. He wanted me to know the world. After three and a half years, he told me, 'Go home, have a normal life and help people with what you have learnt.'

Q: Now we live as much in the virtual world as in the physical world. Teachings of gurus are available on the internet at the click of the mouse, and there's no need to undertake arduous journeys to remote ashrams of spiritual guides. What about the personal touch of a guru?

Spiritual evolution is individual, it cannot be a mass phenomenon with meditation technique franchises.

The seers of Vedanta, the rishis, saw that consciousness is the source of the entire cosmos. It manifests in all the forms we behold, every form we can think of or can possibly conceive of. You and I are just one aspect of the 'supreme seamless continuous reality'. When all grasping stops, when the mind is still, then you touch spirituality.

I am interested in deeper aspects, not religious rituals. I want to be a true human, *Manav*, so I chose to retain the common M as my name. Although my *parampara* (tradition) is kriya yoga, I propound satsang as it cuts across all barriers. That's important.

Live Like a Guest

Q: All our scriptures teach us about the impermanence of existence, but how can those words be truly understood by the heart? The walls of my house are solid, there are people to love and places to see.

Today, I am here. Tomorrow, I'll pack my bags and go there. If you can live like a guest, in the knowledge that all this is not permanent, then you can enjoy everything. Enjoy the beauty of life, the beauty of this earth. Keep your eyes, nose and ears open, let it flow in through your sight, scent and hearing.

Millions of cells in our body die, and new ones appear without us being conscious of it. Our bodies are impermanent, life is impermanent. But, somehow, we believe the impermanent will exist permanently. Look round you. Pandemics can, and do, decimate populations. Understand that anything can you have can be taken away at any moment. Tsunamis, hurricanes, earthquakes can wipe out palaces and entire cities in a day.

Q: What are we working for if there is no incentive to create a better life for ourselves and our families, a beautiful home and more opportunities?

The moment you zoom in and want to possess it, you will find that beauty itself has fled. The world is full of beguiling things, but things are beautiful in their own place. Beautiful flowers, beautiful women, beautiful ornaments, everything is beautiful because it is out there, moving and flowing, but that does not mean I must put them in my pocket. That's when the trouble starts.

We need a few bare necessities of life. Food, clothes and a roof over your head to protect you from the sun and the rain. As for the rest, let it flow. Don't get caught up in possessiveness. A velvet blanket is still only a blanket.

Q: Surely, we possess our own bodies? As a woman, or man, in the world, how can we not cherish ourselves? How can one believe that our bodies are a mere arena for cells living and dying?

You are known in this world by your name and form. That's how others recognize you with their five senses. But deep down within you, you sense that you are not the name and form by which others refer to you. Why do people feel they are not old even when the mirror reflects a senior citizen? Because you sense the immortal soul in you.

The yogi, or the one anchored in the divine, exists in a different space, and is living in-between. Such a Being knows the reality behind name and form and understands the impermanence. He or she carries the fragrance of that other space when interacting with the world. The emotions are different, but that doesn't mean that person is less caring.

The correct expression is manifested at the right time in such a Being who interacts with others on their level, talks and jokes with them according to the level of their understanding but does not over-step a boundary, and also knows where that boundary is drawn.

The Quality of Gratitude

Q: What is the importance of expressing gratitude?

Gratitude is not something that can be expressed in words. It is a feeling that arises without reason. Gratitude is not felt towards any single person or any particular situation, but everything in general. It is a feeling of thankfulness for just being alive; when a leaf moves, when a breeze blows, when the sun rises, we are grateful to everything and everyone. That's gratitude.

Gratitude is a feeling that comes from within. It is not cultivated. Describing gratitude in words is not possible.

On the Divine Self

Mysteries of God

Q: The search for God goes on: mystics in the desert, monks in caves, Himalayan rishis, all seek Him, and some discover Him, but we still we don't know exactly. Why is God hidden?

God is not hidden. That's the idea we've been given, cooked and served to us on a plate. In the Upanishadic concept there is divinity, but it is not an anthropomorphic projection of the human being.

From the Upanishadic point of view the entire manifestation is the Supreme Being. Everything is Brahman. What that means is IT is in us, as well as in the world around us. The soil in which the seed is planted is divine because it urges the seed to grow. The little sapling becomes a mighty tree. That in itself is a great wonder. What other miracles are we looking for? In the Hindu system, God is not worshipped separately but is manifest in everything—in the tree, in the stone, and in every other single thing. He is present in all of His manifestations. There is nothing at all to which you can point and can say, 'That is not God.'

Q: But how can we understand the Unknowable?

God is beyond all images.

Cave men also had concepts about thunder and lightning, and it came from human insecurity. When you are in awe of something you feel there is a Mighty Being behind the phenomenon. And so Might became important. It becomes a chain of power—the subject fears the might of the king, the king fears the emperor, the emperor fears God.

God is not a being to fear before whom you must cower and plead. That concept allowed a certain necessary law and order to be maintained through fear and authority.

If you say that you converse with God, in your mind you are conversing with the image you have made of the Supreme Being. That does not mean to deny divinity.

All our definitions of the Supreme Being stop short. We must evolve and go back to the Source, and only then will we understand that we are no different from THAT. Then we will have no desires left to be fulfilled. After that, what is there left to ask for?

The *Yoga Sutras* are about evolving from man to superman. About exceeding our limits. The next step we need to take is towards spiritual evolution.

Q: We pray when in difficulty and ask for solutions. Who will help us?

If you are having difficulties in your life, it is no good theorizing whether God has created them or not. Just take a good hard look at the situation and ask, 'how can I solve it?' That should be your attitude.

God is neutral. He is not involved in activities. There is an opposite view that God is sitting out there and we are here, and that we are suffering and crying before him, and that He has to help. But if the Supreme Being has to solve your problem, and the solution conflicts with someone else's problem, then whose problem will He solve? My problem solved could create a problem for my neighbour. Would that be divine justice?

Examine the situation, study it carefully, draw a graph of action, and take matters into your own hands. Make a firm resolve to solve it.

Q: What is the importance of religion in our age?

There can be no full stops in man's search for the Divine. So many prophets and rishis and holy books have given us teachings, but we cannot say that any one sage or any one work is definitive. There are so many religions, some which enshrine God, and others who do not even acknowledge God. We cannot say one is superior to the other, or that one is right and one is wrong. Let us not be prejudiced.

We are all human beings with the same body, senses and minds. The ancient teachings of Vedanta tell us to purify our minds and find the truth. Look for the reality behind the material world. It's like the screen on which a film is being projected—there is a blank screen, and then there are the flickering, moving images being projected on to that blank screen. Ask yourself, 'Who am I? What is my relationship to the world?' Find your own truth.

Q: How can we touch God, how can we meet God?

The Kena Upanishad, after saying that this is the reality, or Brahman, states, 'That which cannot be seen by the eye, it cannot be heard by the ear, it cannot be described in words. That is the Brahman the mind finds difficult to grasp because the mind is limited.'

At the end of each sloka it is stated, 'That Alone is the Truth. Please understand O Disciple that it is the Truth. Nothing that you worship here.'

That's a clear statement. The all-Pervading divinity can be worshipped in any form because each one is a manifestation of the all-pervading. It can also be understood as being without form. The problem arises if we say that this form is better than that form.

The all-pervading being pervades everything, including pleasure and pain, it is present in the difficulties, and it is also present in the non-difficulties. It is everywhere. The Malayalam poet in Hari Nama Sankirtanam sings of the bliss of realizing that the mind is the eye of the physical eye, and consciousness is pure awareness that is aware of the mind and thoughts. It is all-pervading and is not confined to one body. It expresses itself through the brain, but it can also express itself without physical organs.

Anybody who has touched it knows it is everywhere. There's no place where it is not. The Upanishads say *chit* is the nature of pure awareness, not awareness of this, or awareness of that. Just awareness of itself. Awareness has no *gunas*, no attributes. That is called *Kaivalya*. It comes from the root *kevala*. Only One.

In Advaita Vedanta it is the Supreme Brahman which is not doing anything, just sitting and watching.

*Q: '**Atma**' is mysterious and intangible. Does it mean my soul?*

Atma does not necessarily mean soul or spirit. *Atma* means me, myself, I.

Then it came to signify both the inner self and the egotistic I. And *atma* came to be translated as the ego, and also as the soul. These are English words. The original concepts have to be understood in Sanskrit.

We need to remain identified with THAT but must also use our own individual intelligence and discernment. The macrocosm and the microcosm. Otherwise, what's the meaning of evolution?

There is a story about disciples going into a forest where a mad elephant is rampaging. The mahout seated on top of the elephant shouts that all must get out of the way. Everyone runs, except for one disciple, who faces the elephant with arms outstretched, yelling, 'The elephant is Brahman, I am also Brahman'. What happens next? The elephant picks up the man with his trunk and flings him aside. Somehow, he survives.

Later, he complains to his Master, 'You said everything is Brahman, but look what happened to me.'

The Master replies, 'But the mahout sitting on the elephant is also Brahman and he was shouting a warning to get out of the way. It was your stupidity not to run.'

Q: *What is the quality of Grace? How can one evoke Grace in our lives?*

We always want somebody to be blessing us but Grace is blessing per se. It is the essence of the universe.

Grace is present in all places, all the time and in all circumstances. Because our windows are shut, we think about Grace in a completely different way, so we don't experience it. Just open your windows and let it flow in. You do not need to do anything else.

We are alive because of Grace.

Grace is not Doing Something. It is just Being.

Be Your Truth

Q: There is much emphasis on truthfulness in spiritual teachings. Yet the quantum of lies in the world is far greater. How can one know the truth?

If you are really serious about the spiritual path, you have to be entirely truthful. But can we live honestly and be truthful in our dealings? There are worldly matters to deal with too. Satya, truthfulness, is difficult in our modern life where we live with many lies and make-believe. If total transparency can get you into trouble, then it is better to keep quiet instead of telling an untruth.

There are people who are habitual liars, who love to lie, but claim they are looking for the truth. People who are liars may be winners in the short term, but they lose out in the long term. Their soul is far away from the spiritual evolution that we seek, and they are not even aware of that. They gain temporary satisfaction, but not lasting happiness.

Q: Where should we look for lasting satisfaction?

Absolute satisfaction is a dream. You may be satisfied with one aspect of your life but dissatisfied with another aspect. I have met hundreds of thousands of people in my life over the years, and not found a single person who is secure unless he is spiritually settled.

It is a long journey to find the truth, and an adventurous one, but instead of addressing their existential dissatisfaction, people bury it under distractions such as alcohol, parties, unnecessary activity. Alcohol makes them feel free. Then they emerge from the fumes to find that nothing has changed.

There have been great sages who have lived in luxurious surroundings, and there have been other sages who lived in poverty. There is not just one single ideal.

A solitary spiritual man with nothing, not even his next meal, seated under a tree, smiling, content, will then face the demands of the many who come to take his blessings. People may arrive in expensive cars to ask a man who has nothing to give them something. Why are they there? They are not satisfied with what they already have. The usual demands are for a better job, a daughter's advantageous marriage, better business, or the boon of a child.

If you don't move out into the unknown, leaving behind your trappings, how will you ever find it? I am talking about the mind, not physical comforts. It is not a question of leaving everything. It is the knowledge that there is no absolute security in this world

Find your own truth. Not somebody else's truth.

Q: Your search for the truth put you in dangerous situations. Were you afraid?

I was nineteen when I secretly left home for the Himalayas, searching for a yogi, searching for my guru. Many times, I felt afraid. Once, I slept in what I thought was a sadhu's cave. On both sides on the way up to Gaumukh Gangotri there are caves, usually occupied by sadhus. Maheshwarnath Babaji had told me to make my way to Gaumukh alone and meet him there. I protested that I had never been there and didn't know how to get there. He said that was precisely the problem, that I had become too dependent upon him. He told me to make a start and left. I don't know where he went.

On one particular night it was getting late and I had nowhere to go, so I entered a cave and decided to spend the night there. It was reeking of bats, or so I thought. I was very tired and was soon fast asleep. It was the night of the full moon and moonlight was flooding in through the cave opening. Suddenly, the light was blocked and it grew dark inside. I was instantly awake and, looking up saw a huge black being blocking the entrance. It's a gorilla, was my first thought. But it was not. I suddenly realized it was a bear. So what do I do? That's what I mean that one must find a solution to the problem facing you. Somewhere, sometime, I had heard that if you are confronted by a bear, then roll over on your stomach, close your eyes and play dead. At the same time, I was praying, I can tell you, silently calling all my gurus and teachers, and sending out signals to everybody else too. I was sure that when I opened my eyes again I would either be in heaven or hell, but no longer on earth. But here I must add that I was not really frightened.

The bear came up to my head, sniffed, made a lot of noise but did not touch me. I waited. Then everything became quiet. I dared not move. It was only when all was silent for a long time that I ventured to turn my head and peep. The cave was empty. I rose and took a good look round but the bear was gone. He must have believed that I was dead, so my ruse had worked. He obviously did not wish to occupy a cave with a dead body in it.

I emerged from the cave and took a good look round. It was very bright because of the full moon, and there was no sight of him. There were several other caves around, but they could all be concealing bears for all I knew. There was no longer any question of sleep, so I sat under a nearby tree and meditated. At dawn, some villagers going past with their goats saw me and there was great commotion. They asked where I had spent the night, and when I pointed to the cave where I had slept, they were shocked. They called me a 'big' yogi, touched my feet and took me to their village. They plied me with milk and food, others came and touched my feet. Apparently, it was impossible to emerge alive after spending a night in that cave. That had been a dangerous experience.

Babaji was already in Gaumukh when I finally got there. He laughed when I narrated the incident to him, and said these things happen to a wandering yogi.

I felt deeply affronted. What if I had died?! He said that I could not have died, it was not time for that since I still had a lot of work ahead of me. He dismissed such incidents with a laugh.

The Inner Journey

Q: Are men at an advantage on the spiritual path? Many spiritual traditions do not give spiritual parity to women or acknowledge that their attainment can be equal to that of a man.

Atma has no sex. There is no gender there.

Men and women are equal on this path. Spiritually, there's no difference between men and women. If both are doing sadhana, both are equal and will reach the same goal.

Among certain religions and sects there is a belief that if a woman has to attain liberation she must be born in a man's body. I think that's a misunderstanding. I feel that means that such a woman may develop some male characteristics, mental characteristics, of course, not physical. When a woman goes deep into spiritual practices she may, after a certain stage, develop some characteristics such as courage, traditionally associated with men. That's a sign that she is moving towards the goal. That's my understanding.

Women have as much freedom to attain liberation as men. There are equal opportunities on both sides, and advantages and disadvantages on both sides too.

Q: What are the main obstacles on the spiritual path?

Fear stops people from committing themselves to the spiritual life because they feel they are giving up so much. That is a misunderstanding.

Young people fear being left behind, but that fear is induced by the society we live in, to which we try to conform.

What matters most is one's own happiness. Externally we may be dependent upon things and feel happy, but deep down we are not. If all the paraphernalia does not give you inner happiness, but instead creates insecurity and fear of loss, then what use is that?

I am not talking about physically selling everything off. It's about an attitude. We are loaded and need to empty that.

A Dzogchen ('Great Perfection' or *Atiyoga*) master had a disciple who had continuously lived with him for twenty-five years, and he complained that nothing was happening to him, that he had not experienced Dzogchen (according to Dzogchen literature it is the path to perfect enlightenment). The master was silent. Then one day he said, 'You see that hill over there? Take this big gunny bag, fill it with rocks until it is stuffed, stitch it up. Pick it up, put it on your shoulders and walk up the hill. I'll meet you there under the tree.' The bag was very heavy and difficult to lift but he placed it on his shoulders and started walking up. He was exhausted by the time he reached the top.

The master, meanwhile, had quickly reached the top on his horse and was waiting for him. The disciple said, 'Master, I want to throw off this weight.' The Master said, 'Yes, throw it.' The disciple threw the load off his shoulders and heaved a sigh of relief. He went and sat down, leaning against the tree, and said. 'I know now what you mean. I think I have Dzogchen.'

Change the attitude of your mind and implement your resolutions. We need peace, happiness, tranquillity, freedom. When you realize that is the core you need and want, then you are comfortable whether the paraphernalia is there or not. The mind has to learn to be free.

Q: Is it really possible to serve both man and monad?

You can both live in this world and attain spiritual fulfilment at the same time, provided you know the rules and regulations, and there are dos and don'ts. One of the first rules is ahimsa, non-violence. Not as a moral concept, but as a practice. That means not to cause injury to other living beings, not just physical injury but also mental injury. You may wish to take revenge, but the past is over and done with. Move forward. It's not easy, but it is possible. Another is satya, truthfulness. *Asthya* is another one. Try not to covet another person's property. Do not have the attitude that you also want everything that others have. And *brahmacharya*, which does not mean forced celibacy. The great rishis in hermitages were married and had families.

People are afraid to take even the first step on the spiritual path. I urge you to take that important step one. Know that if I have realized it, you can too. Accept the hypothesis, but examine it, and figure out for yourself by

111

doing sadhana. Sadhana is not about reaching somewhere. One purifies the vessel to make it fit to receive the flow of grace and knowledge. Sadhana is merely a method passed on by a spiritual teacher who has practised it himself, and who customizes it for the student.

Q: What are the demands of sadhana?

Have a daily schedule, otherwise, success is not possible. The mind runs in various directions all our lives and we need to bring it back and move in one direction.

Patanjali in the *Yoga Sutras* says there is only one way to make the mind one-pointed. Practise, practise, practise for a long time, and that's the only way to clear up your mind, to make it positive and free it from negativity.

The hours of dawn and dusk are very important for any kind of spiritual practice. Both these times are called *sandhya* because they are the coming together of the darkness and light.

Q: What is the true nature of spirituality?

It is an independent soul that comes into the body. Nobody belongs to anybody. Everybody comes and goes alone. Relationships disappear with death. It is like moving from one room to another. The body changes shape and gets a new facade.

I was very attached to my mother, but I left for the Himalayas without telling her. How many mothers have there been in my many cycles of existence?

Who am I? Nothing belongs to me. If I feel that my body belongs to me, it is like the clothes I take off and place on the hanger. I remember some of my past lives. In some I was a woman, in others a man, but the inner self has no sex.

The individual soul is reborn, it is embodied. It begins to distinguish itself as a separate being and appear to itself as an individual. Without that, the soul cannot think or recognize itself. We have to help those who are part of this cycle.

Earning a living, going through the travails of mundane worldly existence is a necessary step to learn about spiritual consciousness. If the world were a complete obstruction to the attainment of higher realms of spiritual evolution, then the Supreme Being would not have created it at all. Working does not disturb your mind; it is expectations that disturb your mind. The world exists around us and in our minds to help make us grow and become complete.

Q: What's the difference between soul and spirit?

People generally use the same word for spirit and soul but these are English words. The language in which these metaphysical concepts came into our consciousness is

Sanskrit, and the word is *atma*. Each of us has that small indestructible spark in us. It is important to discuss the root of the word in Sanskrit. Some say it is mind stuff, but it is not. It is the potential to be aware. Be awake.

Upanishads are written in Sanskrit and are largely non-denominational. Vedanta attempts to understand reality in the present moment. This reality is all-pervading, it is also there in you and I. Human beings have the special capacity to become fully conscious and aware of that. The Upanishads say *chit* is the nature of pure awareness. If we imbibed some of the essence of the Upanishads, then we could see the supreme reality everywhere and work for the common good, instead of being self-serving. Become human first, otherwise one cannot be spiritual.

The Upanishads say, after analysis, pure consciousness is that which witnesses everything inside and outside. The rishis discovered that happiness, complete fulfilment, is available to every human being independent of anything outside, and it's just that the search has to be reversed from looking outwards to looking within.

When you say spirit, it means the ultimate, all-pervading reality, and the individual soul which is a spark of that. The spirit is never born, never dies. It is always there.

When the soul realizes it is a spark of the spirit, then you see it in yourself, and also wake up to the fact that nowhere is it not present. It is all-pervasive.

In its totality, it is never separate. It is one.

That is why it is called a new birth on the spiritual path. Not another physical birth, but it is like a child learning to stand up, stumbling and falling, and learning to readapt to the world. Learning afresh how to communicate with the world. In the beginning, it is a dilemma.

You call it spirit because it is not physical, but that's not the right word. Consciousness is pure consciousness, and you cannot call it either soul or spirit. It means many things. It is the nature of *chit*.

Consciousness also means *sakshi*. The witness. The all-pervading consciousness is witness to everything that happens. It appears to participate but does not participate. Find the witness in yourself. Now. Not tomorrow. Today. Right now.

The Upanishads

Q: Could we talk a bit about the Upanishads?

The Upanishads are not a doctrine but are in the form of an open discussion between teacher and disciple. The teacher does not pretend to know everything. When young men would go to a rishi, he would say, 'Stay with me for three months and I will teach you if I know.' That is the depth of the Upanishads.

A dialogue is very important. *Samvad.* It presupposes that the important part comes at the end of the dialogue, not before. At the end we can reach some sort of conclusion, or if not a conclusion, at least another way of looking at things. What comes out of a dialogue can be known only at the end, after the dialogue is over.

When we sit together for a dialogue, we are equal. Even if somebody has had great spiritual experiences, when you have a dialogue you have to descend to an equal footing.

If someone is set in their ways and cannot open up the mind but thinks 'this is the only right way', then there are difficulties. Then that is not a dialogue. One can remain at one's station, but look at the good points of others too, and for that you need an open dialogue.

Q: You mentioned higher knowledge and lower knowledge. Surely knowledge is just knowledge?

Upanishads say there are two types of knowledge. One is the ordinary knowledge; the other is the higher knowledge.

All science, literature, philosophy, invention, everything like that falls within the realm of lower knowledge. In fact, when the rishis give a list of lower knowledge, it starts with Rig Veda, Yajur Veda, Sama Veda, which we think of as higher knowledge.

Higher knowledge is that by which one finds the absolute truth. Whatever you study, if it does not lead to truth and unity, and to expand and embrace everyone else, because finally everybody is one, if that does not happen, then it is lower knowledge. Not that lower knowledge should be discarded.

Only when you live with other people can you measure yourself. You have to find and reach a tranquil state of mind which is not affected by joy and sorrow, and remains unmoved by insult and praise. Short or long periods of solitude are necessary, but the higher knowledge has to be practiced in the busy world where you interact with other human beings.

Upanishads are the essence of the ancient teachings, the essence of the Vedas. But it is not other-worldly teaching. My master Maheshwarnath Babaji would say: If you're alone in a cave, meditating for twenty years, and declare you are free of jealousy, anger and so on, who is there to get angry with? Of whom can you be jealous if you're living alone?

Learn to remain steady and sane in the midst of interaction with others, otherwise it is hard to develop in the spiritual realm.

Q: Are the Upanishads about human psychology?

The Upanishads are vast and expansive. Whichever way you approach them, you will always pick up something different. The treasure is in your heart and the Upanishads are a pointer to that treasure.

Philosophy and metaphysics are worked out in Upanishads. We cannot confine it only to psychology. The psychological parts are the yoga darshanas[1] and also the *sankhya* darshana[2] teachings.

Many jewels are scattered about in the Upanishads. One has to go deep into the ocean before one can find the pearl.

---

[1] One of the six darshanas in Hinduism, or systems of philosophy, that have an ancient history. According to yoga darshana, the goal of life is union of the self with the Self, which is the state of self-realization.

[2] *Sankhya* is one of the six darshanas of philosophy. It creates an understanding of the dual realism of the eternal spirit (purusha) and matter (*prakriti*). It has a viewpoint on the creation of the world and the evolution of mankind.

Q: The Bhagavad Gita has been read and interpreted over the past two thousand years by very different generations. What is the yoga of the Gita?

In India, we have the wonderful scripture of the Bhagavad Gita, which is also an Upanishad. It is in the Bhagavad Gita that Sri Krishna manifests as the guru, the Jagat Guru.[3]

It is stated at the end of every chapter of the Gita that is a yoga e.g. Bhakti, Gyana, Karma yoga. The Gita is a synthesis of different yogas.

Arjuna asks Krishna, 'What are the qualities of a great yogi?'

Sri Krishna states that certain characteristics of the heart are key qualities of a great yogi. There are other signs as well, such as:

One who has control over his emotions and senses. The more perfect the control, the higher the attainment of that yogi. All humans fall prey to the temptations of sense organs, and you can indulge them to some extent, but don't allow them to run away with you.

One who maintains tranquillity and peace in the midst of changing circumstances. In this world of dualities, you will inevitably encounter both highs and lows.

One who has concern for all living beings in his or her heart, and works for the welfare of all. Love,

---

[3] Literally means 'guru of the universe'.

compassion and understanding matter in life. That is part of Bhakti yoga.

You should select those parts of religion that encourage brotherhood, love and compassion, and build a society that appreciates these values. Help to create an altruistic concern for the welfare of all other human beings.

If we can pick up the jewels, then we will have made a crown fit for a universal being.

Q: Is Krishna leela an unfolding of a divine play? Are we indeed mere spectators? Is it even possible to observe one's life as a spectator without getting caught up in the emotions? Is there a shorter and easier way to surrender?

When we speak of Krishna Leela and Sri Krishna dancing with thousands of *gopis*[4] simultaneously, that is a divine concept. It is the path of surrender. It is not to be interpreted in the ordinary social way. Krishna is the living divine in their hearts.

Surrender is not an easy path. It happens only when you understand there is truly no other way, when you have exhausted all possible schemes and you still cannot free yourself. Then you realize you placed far too much importance on your personal effort and know that the

---

[4] *Gopi* is a Sanskrit word that means 'female cowherd', 'wife of a cowherd', 'milkmaid' or 'female guardian'. In Hinduism, it typically refers to the cow-herding girls and women who were devoted to Krishna.

intellectual structure you built up—that little mind of mine—cannot solve the problem. Drop the sense of doership: I'm doing this, I'm doing that. Only when you let that go can you truly surrender.

Surrender is a big thing. It comes very late in the Bhagavad Gita, not at the beginning. It comes only after Arjuna has been granted the vision of Sri Krishna, the darshan of Sri Krishna, as Vishwaroopa. It is only after that that Arjuna totally surrenders to Sri Krishna.

Q: What is the importance and relevance of Sanskrit today?

Sanskrit is a root language of India, but it has been neglected. It is a unifying language.

Mantra is the Raft

Q: What is the value of a mantra? How does mantra **japa**[5] *benefit the* **sadhak**[6]*?*

Mantras turn negative vibrations into more positive vibrations. That is the advantage of chanting mantras. The sound has two parts to it: there is the meaning of the sound and there is the vibration of the sound.

Nama japa is the easiest way to keep continuous remembrance of the divine in today's world. Some prefer the abstract way of engaging the mind in nothingness, but that is not easy to do.

Some mantras, when properly chanted, especially the Gayatri, can penetrate the waking, dreaming and deep sleep states. Which means that it is then reflected in all states of your consciousness, and it affects both the inner and the outer. If it enters into deep sleep, then rest assured your entire personality has been changed.

The Gayatri, from the Rig Veda, is one of the most ancient mantras in the world. The Goddess Gayatri is also called the Mother of the Vedas.

---

[5] The practice of repeating the same mantra continuously until it becomes a natural, fluid part of a meditation practice.
[6] One who follows a form of sadhana, spiritual practice, which leads to self-realization.

Rishi Vishwamitra (Friend of the Universe) is the rishi of the Gayatri Mantra:

Oṃ bhūr bhuvaḥ svaḥ; tat savitur vareṇyaṃ; bhargo devasya dhīmahi; dhiyo yo naḥ prachodayāt

A rough interpretation of the Gayatri Mantra reads as follows:

Meditate on the glory of the Creator of this universe. Worship Him. He is the embodiment of all Wisdom and Light, the destroyer of all sin and ignorance. May He illumine my mind

If you truly concentrate on *nama japa*, then your mind will be absorbed in the sound, and become quiet. The disturbances of the mind have to be calmed and quietened down before creating the possibility of moving to higher levels until you are linked to the cosmic consciousness. It has to be done step by step.

Q: What does it mean to respect the mantra?

A sacred chant carries the energy of the cosmos, and that affects your body. A mantra creates the sense of an armour of protection around your body.

It is important to get the mantra from one who has chanted it and attained *siddhi*[7] in that mantra, which means that he has attained whatever had to be attained ie the fruit of chanting that particular mantra. Of course, you can pick up *nama japa* from a book, but that's not the same thing. When a spiritual teacher gives you a mantra, he will first look to find the right mantra for you. It will not be just any mantra at all but will be specific. When he gives you a mantra that he has understood and experienced for himself, then, apart from the words, he will put a certain energy into it. That's an important point to note. If you are a proper recipient of that mantra, then it has a certain effect on you.

Once you are given a mantra, you must respect it.

Q: When is it the right time to chant your given mantra?

Chanting after doing pranayama and meditation gives better results. If you chant it superficially then it will not be effective.

Fix a time to sit down and chant it. You can continue chanting it as you go about your daily work, like a repetitive drone inside, until one day you will feel great joy in your

---

[7] Complete understanding (siddhis are powers over subtle forces that a yogi has acquired).

heart. That enjoyment will become permanent after some time.

It is good to chant audibly because the mind tends to wander. The sound draws your attention back to it. Silent chanting means that other sounds will enter your ears and your attention will shift there since we use our sense organs all the time. You can chant silently when the mind becomes steady.

Q: What is the significance of AUM?

What is infinite is not easy to grasp in words. It is not reachable by our five senses.

Then how does one touch Brahman? The sound of AUM is an audible link to the inexpressible, the indestructible.

Beej akshara is a seed letter and very powerful sound, very powerful mantra. AUM, or *pranava*, is the greatest of all.

The Brahman cannot be touched by our five senses, the infinite is not easy to grasp in words, even though every one of us has a small spark of the indestructible in us. AUM is a pure sound from ancient India, not linked to any denomination. A primeval, universal sound that links us to the soundless.

AUM needs a lifetime to explain.

The Lotus Blooms in You

Q: Why is the lotus such an important spiritual symbol in Hinduism? And in Buddhism?

The lotus is important in the ancient Indian scriptures, including in Kundalini yoga.[8] It is a great symbol of expanding consciousness.

When you see a lotus bud it is closed. Then, slowly, it begins to expand. It has a very subtle fragrance. The fragrance is so subtle that normal human beings cannot get it, but bumblebees know. You need to reach the level of subtlety before you get the fragrance of it.

Gods hold *padma* (lotus) in their hands.

Plexuses in the human system are called chakras and each one is visualised as a lotus.

The padmaasana that you use for meditating is the lotus pose.

The lotus grows best in muddy water but when it blooms it is pure and clean. Even if you put a drop of water on it, that does not stick but flows down. Live like that in the world, be pure, don't let the mud stick to you.

---

[8] Kundalini yoga is the system of meditation and practices to awaken the latent female energy coiled up at the base of the spine, the kundalini energy, to achieve self-realization.

Flame of Aspiration

Q: You give importance to lighting a **dhuni**. *There are many hymns to the divine agni, or sacred fire, in the Vedas. The Hindu marriage is sanctified by the sacred fire, which bears holy witness. Why is fire so significant in ancient Indian spiritual tradition, and even today?*

Fire is a great symbol of the Spirit. The ancient rishis asked, 'Where was this fire before it came out?' The answer is 'it was inside you but was made to manifest.' The Vedas and Upanishads have compared rubbing a dry stick against another dry stick to lighting the spiritual fire. Two dry sticks are required.

Gorakhsha Shataka[9] says, 'through constant pranayama when all the liquids of the body are dried', which means when all the negative qualities have been removed, 'then two dry sticks that rub together create a spark. When the mind has been made absolutely clear and dry, has no more wetness in it, when such a mind meets another mind like that, the inner spark is ignited by the teacher.'

The Naths have an agni meditation where you sit before the *dhuni*. I did it with Babaji, sitting face to face, looking at the fire. That is beautiful, especially

---

[9] An early hatha yoga text, written in about the 10th century in the tantra tradition.

if you meditate at night. Babaji could send the flame up when he wished to, or the flame came down if he wanted that. He taught me to open my eyes wide and watch the flame, then to close my eyes and visualize the flame inside. It actually burns off many remainders of our past.

Fire has a life of its own. It relates to you in a particular way when you sit in front of the *dhuni* for long periods and meditate. There is no image in fire, yet it is very potent and your attention gets concentrated there.

Q: Do all sadhus and wandering yogis give equal importance to fire?

It has been the custom in India for thousands of years for wandering spiritual seekers and teachers, especially among the Naths, to light a *dhuni*. Wherever Naths go, they light a *dhuni*, which is a small pit in which a fire is lit and kept burning. They take a few ashes from the *dhuni* and rub it on their bodies.

When yogis lived in forests and Himalayan caves, lighting a fire was a difficult task, achieved by rubbing two dry sticks together. The *dhuni* protected their bodies from extreme climates, a tea kettle could be boiled on it and chapatis were cooked in it. At night, the fire would protect them from wild animals.

Q: Is fire a metaphor for spiritual life? Can its symbolic use help the seeker on the path to spiritual realization?

The outer fire helps to light the inner fire of desire for spiritual fulfillment. Only a fire can burn up everything, you cannot wash away desires with water. For spiritual seekers, it is important to light the inner fire that reduces every other desire to ashes. What remains is the eternal satisfaction, with nothing more to be gained, nothing to be lost either, because you have deliberately burnt everything else to nought. That is the fire to light in the heart, otherwise your sadhana will not succeed.

Fire is also a symbol of desire, and what sort of desire that is, is up to you. Igniting any desire inside requires fire. When you meet someone you were once in love with, you say my old flame, not my old water. Some are consumed by the fire of anger, hatred, greed, lust, envy and ambition.

Fire also is a constant reminder of our final end at the cremation ground. Babaji said that when you eat food, remember that time is eating you. Time consumes us, burns us all to ashes. Time does not spare anybody, and nobody can halt it.

A flame always burns upwards. It doesn't go downwards. It is a symbol of the Kundalini fire that burns inside, and through deep meditation lifts your consciousness to higher realms. The spirit always has the aspiration to go up and up.

Q: Could you explain a bit about the Nath Panth, the Nath tradition to which you belong? How did it start, what are the core precepts?

The Nath Panth, or *sampradhaya*, according to old texts, started with someone we refer to as Adinath, the First Nath. Adi means First.

We consider Sri Guru Babaji to be the founder of the Kriya Yoga system, although that existed many hundreds of years ago. We don't know where he learnt it. He taught it to some disciples.

Traditionally, there are 108 *kriyas*.[10] Sri Guru Babaji picked up a few and taught them, and it all started with Babaji. In *Autobiography of a Yogi*, Paramahansa Yogananda refers to him as Mahaavatara Babaji, the first time someone wrote about him in English. In Nath textbooks, he is referred to as Sri Guru Babaji.

I am also a Nath. My connection is that I learnt *kriya* from Sri Maheshwarnath Babaji, who was a direct disciple of Sri Guru Babaji. My guru named me Madhukarnath, and I became M. Madhurkarnath means 'one who has tasted honey'. Madhu is also a name of Sri Krishna.

Nath yogis are usually wanderers and don't stay in one place. Internal practices include many kinds of *kriya*. They have some external characteristics too, from which I am

[10] Techniques or practices within a yoga discipline designed to speed up spiritual progress.

exempt, like *chimta* or tongs, *trishul* or the trident, and two big rings in their ears, and they light a fire every evening wherever they go. My guru said I could light a *dhuni* twice a year, on Guru Poornima and Shivratri days.

On Liberation and Death

All Will Meet Death

Q: Why is death so frightening?

You fear death because you fear loss. But it is only the ego which doesn't want to let go and which fears the loss. You are the one who has built up that ego, filled it with desires, wishes and objects.

You fear to be parted from your near and dear ones. Of course, death creates a void in a family. We feel their absence. It alters the family structure. But death is inevitable.

The illusion is that life will be a smooth, beautiful, continuously happy movement. That is not so. The truth is that life is full of ups and downs. Full of dualities. Fleeting joy is often replaced by sorrow, but that sorrow also disappears. The problem is that we think that all this is permanent when it is all an ever-changing, impermanent movement. There can be a little sunshine of happiness, but then the sun sets, as all suns in all universes set at some time or other. So, there can be a ray of happiness, followed by the shadow of sorrow. Up and down, up and down, and that's how the ferry boat of existence continues its turbulent journey.

You grieve to lose anything at all. That preoccupies your mind from the time that it registers the world at birth, to the time of physical death.

Q: How can we easily come to terms with the reality of death? We see people die all around us, beloved family members or strangers in distant parts, but we don't like to dwell upon death.

When Adinath dances his *Tandava Nritya*,[1] he shatters all images. He destroys images that we have created, and without destroying the old, nothing new can come up. Death too destroys the old, the calcified and the fossilized things. Every day we must prepare for death.

And every day we do die in some measure. Millions of cells die in our bodies, old habits die, circumstances pass away.

---

[1] The *Tandava* refers to Lord Shiva's vigorous dance that is the catalyst for the cycle of creation, preservation and dissolution.

Every night we pass through a small death when we sleep, called *susupti*. Then you don't know who you are, or where you are. There is no inner or outer recognition of yourself. Death too annihilates your personality, but you are afraid of death. Nobody wants to die.

The billionaire and the beggar are both equal in sleep. In death too they are equal, the king and the mendicant, male and female and everyone else. Your identity is annulled in sleep, yet nobody is afraid of sleep. Everybody wants it.

You don't fear loss when you go to sleep because you're confident of waking up in the morning to enjoy all your possessions. But who knows if you will wake up? Nobody knows.

Sleep deprivation is supreme torture and can drive a person mad. Deep sleep is blissful. One of the words used to describe *susupti* is *swaraga*. In the Gayatri mantra the *bhu bhuva swa* refers to the waking consciousness, dream consciousness and then *swa* is the short form of *swaraga*.

In that split second between sleep and waking up, you are happy, before the mind kicks in and worries you, and tells you that you are incomplete. And everyone wants to be happy. Sleep takes you back to your original essence, the inner you. Your true self is a blissful, non-corporeal being. Blissful and complete in itself. For happiness, you don't need things from the outside.

Q: Death is never part of our plans. It seems far away, somewhere in the distant future. What is it in us that refuses to accept the reality?

It could be that the mind refuses to die. It does not want to give up pleasures but wishes to enjoy them endlessly. That becomes its identity, and it refuses to let go of all that it is attached to. Such a mind cannot be as free as the wind because it is entangled in pleasures and become dependent on enjoyment for its existence.

There is a deep-rooted feeling within you that you are not going to die. That you will exist forever. The Upanishads say you believe that because, deep in your subconscious, you know there is some entity in you which will survive the death of the body. Your subconscious has an inkling that is what may be your true identity.

The four *Mahavakyas*[2] guide us on the journey from gross physical body to the astral body and lead us to the causal body. These great sentences teach us to be awake. Just as the Buddha was the Awakened One. The Upanishadic *Mahavakyas* teach us the unity of the individual atman with the Supreme Brahman.

---

[2]   Great Sentences. Also known as Sacred Utterances or Great Contemplations. Four *Mahavakyas* are commonly known, and they include: *TAT TVAM ASI* (You are THAT); *AHAM BRAHMAN ASMI* (I am Brahman/Divine).

Don't be afraid of death. It is only a misunderstanding that you are the body.

You are much more than you think you are. The conflicts in you are artificial. Get rid of the divisions and conflicts, then you will understand you are THAT. That you are already free. Find your freedom.

You are consciousness. You are pure awareness. You are the light.

Feel Your Freedom

Q: What is true freedom? Political, philosophical and spiritual freedom. Is there a natural urge in us to seek freedom? But we also crave security and comfort and have a great need to belong somewhere.

Most people do not desire freedom. They desire to be transferred from an iron cage to a golden cage. But that's still a cage. First, recognize that you are bound. Many are bound but think they are free. To understand bondage is the first step. Study the bondage. See the world clearly. If the chains are golden, we are happy. Only if the chains are made of iron do we complain.

We set forth to find freedom, but almost always end up enslaved, conditioned and bound by various factors, including insecurity and desire. People like security. Handcuffs can be made of gold, copper or iron. These are not physical chains. It's all in the mind.

Wanting to be free is an in-built instinct in all human beings. We want to break the chains. We want to fly, to soar. Even in our minds we want to break out of limitations. It is a natural desire. If you lock up a small child in a room with lots of toys and TV, that child will still want to get out.

Chains are used to bind but are also used for decoration, especially gold chains. But if you look at the structure, the chain is empty. Only in a small portion, volume-wise, is there some material. The rest is empty. So, even in enslavement, even when you are in chains, know that there is an emptiness.

The world has a lot of burdens of sorrow to carry, but you can find the freedom within. You can live in this world with family and associates and still be free. It is an attitude of the mind. Ultimately that's what is going to help you.

External things are temporary. And they are in constant motion.

Q: Is freedom not frightening? To be free, but alone, can be hard to cope with. It is harder for women because of our traditions, and because it has been a man's world for thousands of years. How can a woman free herself from the golden cage?

That applies to all human beings. Women's chains are different, and men's chains are different, that's all. Loneliness is the nature of the mind. Just replace the software. What is inside us is already complete. We may have a nagging feeling we are complete in ourselves, but don't know how to get there. Instead, we look for completeness outside.

If freedom seems frightening that's because you have never experienced true freedom. It's not frightening. The fear of freedom is because the 'I' is there. You fear the loss of identity, therefore you choose to remain in the prison of your mind.

By seeing the mother, the baby first recognizes himself or herself as 'I'. The baby is in darkness in the mother's womb for ten months. Then the same womb muscles that protected and controlled it, push the baby out into freedom, into the world. The baby sees the light, and sees the other. Birth is a beautiful metaphor.

The whole movement of the world is towards completeness. The energy in us is the manifestation of completeness. Understand that it is possible. Turn your gaze in and look for the energy within. Realize the completeness inside you, then you will go to the source. Do not waste any time. Move swiftly towards completeness.

Q: How can one get out of the grooves of one's habits and behaviour patterns? To become free of one's mental conditioning? We have a self-image of who we are, how we must look, speak, behave towards others. That's our identity. If we break free of that, we might lose everything.

Patterns are the problem. One needs to study oneself. Only when you understand where you are headed and say, 'I need to get out', then you can change. Realization is not possible if you run away or avoid it. Instead, look at yourself carefully.

The most important pattern is memory. The past. You need to get out of that before you can see the present. The truth you seek is always in the present. It has to be now. Otherwise, it is no use to us.

Many of our problems exist because we get stuck with what happened in the past. The mind plays tricks on us. Only when you understand that it is all part of memory, an old recording, can you can work to stop it.

One way is to substitute the past with what we have now so that the past is cleared out. Then there's no space for the mind to ruminate over what happened earlier. Understand that is not taking you even an inch towards the goal of the freedom you seek.

We believe our thought process is a continuous whole, but they are only links in a chain. One thought comes very fast. We can't measure the speed. It disappears into the past. A new thought comes. That thought goes. Another comes. And so on. It is so fast and continuous that we tend to look at it like a continuous whole. Actually, it is a chain. In some yogic practices, as in some Sufi practices, and in Zen, you have to watch yourself carefully while your thoughts are moving. Of course, the watcher is also a thought.

At some point, you become so absorbed in the watching that you begin to see the gap between the links of the chain of your thoughts. If you open the link, there is emptiness. When you see the gaps, you are free.

Q: Don't you think fear and doubt are useful for self-protection? There are smiling devils out there who exploit others, especially women, who can be more easily enslaved and suffer great abuse. How can one know whom to trust?

Anything can be exploited commercially. That has become the practice. Spirituality can also be exploited commercially.

A true spiritual teacher has nothing to lose if the disciple has doubts. The spiritual field is not one where you should not doubt anything.

A good teacher will create situations where you become free and will ensure that from the beginning. When the churning happens, if it is genuine, what was inside will come out. That's quite natural. It has to come out before it can evaporate. It is the duty of the teacher to say: don't be frightened, don't be defeated, just absorb it. Let it happen till it evaporates, and that requires patience.

Your love and affection for your teacher should not end up in your becoming enslaved with golden chains to the teacher. That will cover the truth. This is an important point. Where there is too much *suvarna* (gold), be careful.

Do not surrender to any human being. That's the last thing you should do. There's no such thing as a perfect human being on earth. In time, you will discover feet of clay. Surrender only to the highest.

Surrender means to understand in humility that you may not always be right. That your limited logic may not have solutions to problems bigger than you can handle. Then let go, be patient and wait. True freedom emerges when the mind is absolutely at peace with itself and with the world. There is divinity in every heart which, in its essence, is peace, tranquillity and happiness. In that waiting, something arrives, and the breeze may come from within.

Q: How far should one go in the quest for freedom? You had secretly left home at nineteen. What drove you to do that?

I realized at some point that I was in a golden cage. My freedom of thought was being interfered with. I wanted to search, to seek. We were very well taken care of at home because ours was an affluent family. My father's greatest regret was that I never joined his construction business, being the only son. But at the age of nine, Maheshwarnath Babaji had put his blessed hand on my head and my spiritual journey began.

For me, it was a one-pointed search, totally compelling, like a fish out of water desperate for water. You cannot induce that or fake it. And you cannot imitate anyone else. That sort of serious search will begin only if it is one-pointed.

I felt there was something else beyond what I knew, something I could not touch by starting out with a belief. I wanted to get out of beliefs and get into the path of inquiry. In the *Yoga Sutras*, Upanishads and the Gita, there is always an inquiry.

If I had kept on worrying that it was going to be terrible, I would never have left home. But I told myself, 'Let me just go, and if I die, then I die.' I missed a few meals, I suffered a bit, but did not die. Actually, it's a grand occasion if you have a meal after missing three or four. I remember I had not eaten for three days and drank water from the river to fill my belly. Then a sadhu offered me a big ripe mango. I have never eaten such a tasty mango! I was totally satisfied and did not need to eat anything else that evening. But the sadhu took me to a Vaishnavite ashram further down the river. When they finished their pooja, they offered me food.

The beginning of a spiritual journey is dissatisfaction with the status quo. Fortunately, those who have experienced it say it is joyful, blissful and infinite. The speed of the journey may depend on the road you take and the gems of experiences you carry from the past. There are innumerable ways to reach that. Some paths suit some people but others don't, so make sure it is your path. It can be difficult to figure that out, and that's where teachers can help.

Q: You stepped out into the unknown. What are the pitfalls of the path?

I decided, 'I am walking on this path, and it's a lonely path.' Stick to your spiritual path if you are serious. Make a *sankalpa* (resolve), to do that. Many times, I admit I was afraid. I was also cheated. I learnt to face fear when I set out from home into the unknown. I had my own fears, such as fear of the dark. Later, I had fearful visions and half-visions, terrible and ferocious, alone in the dark Himalayan nights.

The only way to get out of fear is to face it. Look straight at it. I am talking about imaginary fears, not physical dangers. But don't be foolish. Fear is not an illusion. It is a defense mechanism built into our ancient reptilian brain to protect us from danger. It is an intrinsic part of our constitution. If you don't focus on the danger, that would be escapism. Our practical attitude should be to tackle it. You can't say, 'I'll leave it.' At the same time don't get tense and worried.

Q: Is a yogi, a maharishi, an enlightened one, bound in any way? Can such a Being still get upset by difficulties? If there is a permanent state of bliss, surely there are no challenges left.

Do not believe there are no difficulties in a yogi's life, because there surely are. But a yogi is not affected by them because he is free.

It is a very important concept for a spiritual person to free oneself. Freedom, or *swatantrata*, in the spiritual realm is described by different words, as Moksha by the Vedantists, *Kaivalya* by Yogis, and Nirvana by Buddhists.

Moksha. *Kaivalya.* Nirvana. It all has to be done in the body. That is the ancient Indian concept of freedom. It is not an otherworldly philosophy, that when you die you go to heaven. Instead, it says that if you are not free while still in the body, then there's no meaning in that freedom.

Freedom is our birthright. Our true self, the atman, is free and does not need to be freed from anything because it is already *poorna*, complete. Break free of all psychological bondage and realize that your true self was never bound.

On the Past and Future

The Power of Karma

Q: It is said the wheels of justice grind slowly, but they grind fine. Is there really a detailed record kept in the ether of all our thoughts and actions? How can one negotiate through one's life with so much past, hidden, stuff we carry?

Karma is misunderstood. Every action has a reaction. Good or bad actions each have results. Nobody is testing us. Don't blame fate. Don't blame divine dispensation. Don't blame anybody. It is in your hands.

Physically, we are born in certain circumstances and cannot change that. Millions of years of genetic evolution have created a particular combination of genes. Traits have been combined in a particular way in one person. But, after that, we can do a lot to change things. Simply to say it is all the doings of the divine is a defeatist attitude. There's nothing like that.

Q: In India we often hear that it is so-and-so's karma, hence life is good or bad for them and that can't be helped. Is it so mechanical?

You can change things now. If you believe the whole entity was created by a divine power to bring about certain goals, then let me tell you that you also have that divine power within yourself. Whether you know it or not, it is there within you. You can change things now if you want.

That's a great hope that I offer to everybody.

If you're having a problem, then you have created the conditions for it in a previous birth. You don't know it, of course. But change it now so that in the future you don't have to face the same problems. You can't go back and tinker with what you did in the past. That's not possible. The now is more important. At least try. Without trying you cannot say you have failed.

Never accept defeat but consider it as a lesson for you to learn and move forward. Ask anyone who has succeeded. They never turned away because of defeat. Do not ever give up.

Q: What is the way out of the hole one may find oneself in today?

When you face a situation, think, 'How do I solve it?' Look at the situation, draw a graph, and take matters into your own hands. It is no good theorizing whether God created it or not.

Ask yourself, 'How can I perform actions perfectly? Is there a script of my life? Do I have any control?' One is the fatalistic view, where you feel you cannot do anything.

My own view is that if we do have a script, we can try and change that. If everything is pre-destined, then it would just be a blind movement. We do have a script, but we must also act. Pay complete attention to your actions and do not worry about the result. If it goes wrong, then it just does.

Suffering is a cleansing process. Cleanse the soul and set it free. Ultimately everyone wants to be free. Even if you have done something wrong, retribution will not last forever.

The inner spiritual journey is a tough journey but what awaits us at the other end makes it worth undertaking. Do not run away.

Q: Is there an easy route to follow in life given the weight of karma from past eons?

Understand that memories of past wounds and regrets is only a tape playing in our heads. It is not reality. Nowadays, depression has become all too common.

When you get up in the morning, throw open the windows. Say to yourself, 'Let me have a fresh day.' Then you will feel free and light and not carry the heavy burdens of yesterday. Also, tell yourself, 'Let me not see the person in the light of what he or she did yesterday, good or bad.' Even if it was bad, they might have changed today. Some might feel 'Oh, but I won't allow him to change!'

The Upanishads tell us, 'Let go and rejoice!'

The Law of Dharma

Q: What is dharma? How can one ever understand one's individual dharma if it is so personal, depends on very many factors and there is no clear definition?

We are born in different situations, in different locations, and each one has a different expression of dharma, but there is a basic dharma for everyone. Those qualities never change.

Truthfulness, kindness and compassion are fundamentals. The first rule is truthfulness. That's very important in dharma. If you say one thing but your action is the opposite of that then that's *adharma*.[1] Without the quality of truthfulness, you could not trust or believe in anybody in this world. Truthfulness is especially important for leaders, whether political or spiritual. Imagine how it would be if a spiritual teacher tells lies.

Trustworthiness is important. If you don't budge from the truth, you might have some setbacks because the world is contrary, but in the long run those will become achievements.

Dharma also means your activities, your character, your attributes. The way you conduct yourself, especially under pressure. How the mind thinks, what are its principles,

---

[1] A Sanskrit word which means 'what goes against dharma' or, more literally, 'not-dharma'.

good or bad, all of which is normally hidden. What is invisible is more important than the visible. The visible is based on the invisible. We cannot ignore the intangible and dismiss it as not being there, for that is the foundation, the core without which actions would be a nightmare. Hidden thoughts and desires are what manifest through action.

Action reveals what is behind it, the motivation. These are the qualities that define you. We have possessions, and we utilize them to the best of our capacity. There is no need to give up everything, but do acquire things by legitimate means, not by cheating others. That is dharma. People indulge in lies and deception just to possess things. That is *adharma*. And sharing is very important. Share with others even a little bit of what you have.

Q: You say the invisible, the hidden, is as important as manifest action. But who is to know? Who can understand the hidden motivations of cunning and duplicitous people? It's quite common to be cheated out of money or liberty.

There is a record kept in the minutest detail of our lives, our thoughts, our intentions and our deeds, and it is an invisible record. Nobody gets away with anything. This relates to karma. People who lie and cheat may be winners in the short term but they lose in the long term. Their soul is far away from the spiritual evolution that we seek, and they are not even aware of that.

We tend to think that life is only from this birth to this death, but that's a small part of our journey. It is only one bead in a very long garland each one of us has of many, many beads. But we remain focused on this one single bead, worrying and fretting about it, instead of seeing the thread that strings all the beads together. The thread of consciousness of your personal garland stretches way back into the past and far ahead into the future. Call it spirit, call it soul, call it what you will, because words have their own connotations. That is the consciousness because of which we are aware. Awareness is not a chemical substance, it is not corporeal. The awareness is not because of the brain, rather the brain is aware because of the consciousness.

Q: Does dharma mean duty?

You are born in a certain family, and you have relatives by birth. You feel the inner urge to repay them and help them with their difficulties. But attachment makes you fear that you will lose them. If you recognize that anyone can go at any time, then you lose your fear and can work with detachment.

Detachment does not mean you live in a vacuum, because the mind cannot remain blank all the time. Instead, you get attached to something higher. It could be *seva*, service. Somebody may not believe in God, but they may like to do good to others. Their attachment to service detaches them from other little things.

The Pandemic

Q: The coronavirus pandemic created total uncertainty, with people living in intense and prolonged fear, physical, mental as well as financial. How could one cope with that?

The pandemic teaches us that we are all the same. We are all human, whoever we may be. The virus doesn't distinguish between us. It puts us all on common ground. We can be snuffed out at any moment. Everyone has to face death. We don't know who will go when. The reality that life is uncertain and insecure has been shown to us. We are not masters of the universe, we must not exploit the earth, and the time has come now to give back.

Fear comes from the brain. When it circulates in your blood that makes you weak. When you're not afraid, the hormones that circulate in your blood make you powerful and vital. We've gone through a lot of pain and pressure and sorrow. When sorrow strikes, human beings begin to think of higher things. Otherwise, they are quite happy with what they have. One practical way of bringing about change in this time of sorrow is yoga. Yoga can protect your body and increase your resistance. Then you can deal with the situation better, both mentally and physically.

In the coronavirus crisis we have been forced to be locked down for health reasons. People who are outgoing and closely linked to society are desperate about being in enforced isolation for so long. I would suggest to you change the word 'isolation' to 'solitude'. It's a question of how you look at things. From ancient days, people in search of inner growth have imposed solitude upon themselves even though there was no pandemic raging. Great yogis and teachers spent time alone. They deliberately sought solitude in order to focus within, to tame their minds and energy in order to attain high levels of spiritual realization. That cannot be done if one is always talking and travelling and expending energy outwards.

Solitude acquires a spiritual significance. Say to yourself, 'I am going to use the solitude to the best of my advantage.' There is a lot you can sort out which you could not do earlier when you were busy running round.

You can even create your own little solitary cell in your heart, in all our hearts, to which we can retreat when we want.

Music helps us to come to terms with our emotions at difficult times. Spiritual thoughts and religions are all linked to music, and it carries you up there. Music does not need language or words.

As for the practical aspect of suffering, we could try and make our minds more humanitarian and look after others.

Q: What is your message for the youth? The pandemic robbed them of valuable time, and they face an uncertain future with jobs disappearing and economies shrinking. How can they avoid depression and anxiety and face the future with optimism?

My message to the youth is to not take it as a defeat. Use the opportunity to build a new world. Make the blueprints now when you have the time. Think not that you are in isolation, but that you are in solitude. That will help you survive COVID-19 and any other crisis. The pandemic will go away, it cannot remain forever. Everything has to go. When it goes, we might emerge as better people, with better understanding, greater energy and greater possibility to meditate. Meanwhile, take it as a chance to be in solitude and think about serious things. There is no alchemist except your mind, and that can transmute copper into gold.

Spend some time in reading and doing things you could not do before. The lockdown also helped to bring families together. Small children are intelligent and have so much energy, they should have hobbies in the lockdown to keep them engaged.

In the pandemic, economies touched an unprecedented low, but human beings are very resilient. Financiers will aways find the way forward to make the world economy more stable in future. But we can and should become more mindful of how we live. Financial and economic growth should not be at the cost of compassion and goodness. Expansion yes, but not at the cost of human suffering. If you make money, do share some portion of it with those who are under-privileged.

Utilize the opportunity to prepare, to dwell in your own minds and find the essence which is in everyone else too. That is the spirit. Go inside and touch the spirit. Then come together to understand that in essence we are all the spirit.

The young are going to take over the world in future, so say to them, 'Make the most of this time.' Due to the pandemic, we need to create new stories to make connections between the past and future. We have seen how terrible the world can be, and now we have the chance to dream about how to do better in future. The themes of stories may be old, but they need to be dressed up in the new clothes of humanity to suit present and changing circumstances.

Be like the moth that breaks free of the cocoon to become a beautiful, colourful butterfly flying high up in the air.

The New Century

Q: 'Spirituality' has become be a trendy and cool word now. But life has changed beyond all recognition, speeded up by cheap and easy travel, high levels of education and affordable personal computers for all. What is the meaning of true spirituality in our twenty-first century lives?

Today, the problem is that we like to be too much in control of ourselves. We want to be too voluntary. No ordinary mind can make 100 per cent correct decisions. There is conflict the moment you try to become perfect because the mind by its very nature is incomplete. There will always be a lacuna somewhere, and we must live with that knowledge.

Day by day, you need to solve your problems. Society is such that you cannot be completely good or completely bad. God doesn't enter the picture here.

Ask yourself, 'Can I deal with my own mind?' The mind is only an instrument, and you must understand that.

There are many temporary ways you can address it— entertainment, yoga, meditation—but the permanent solution is when your mind is without conflict. We need to work on creating a quiet mind, tranquil, at peace, without distractions, not torn in many directions. That's the journey. There is a difference between being and becoming. At some point when one is mature enough to touch THAT, then you can be just as you are.

If there is great longing in you, then a spiritual guide is not far away, but your heart has to be overwhelmed by that intense longing, just as a starving man craves food and one dying of thirst yearns for water. The person whose heart is flooded by such longing for darshan of the lord, will find that the lord is not far off. He stays near the seeker. It is true disciples who are a rarity.

Q: How can one identify one's guru with certainty?

How will you identify your guide? From his attire? It is not necessary for a guru to have any particular paraphernalia.

I'll tell you a Sufi story about a guru. Somewhere in the Middle East lived a man who was spiritually inclined since childhood, but he was very poor. He saw rich people and wanted that for himself too. He worked hard and earned great wealth. By the time he was fifty, he had everything that money could buy, but no peace, happiness or satisfaction. The tiny lamp of spirituality within him had dimmed but not been extinguished. He called his wife and children and told them of his decision to retire to an oasis, saying 'I shall be on my own and will spend time in spiritual pursuits.' He distributed his business among them. They were happy with the prospect of all that they would receive. He kept a small sum to take with him, and his books. Since he was wealthy, he had forgotten how to even make a cup of tea for himself, so the family searched and found a man in the village who claimed to be a good cook and was prepared to accompany him into the desert.

For seven years, the two men lived by themselves in a hut at an oasis and the man read his books and meditated. But after seven years he felt the need for a Sheikh, a Murshid or Guru. He searched for one and met a man in green robes, with a long beard, green turban and a rosary in his hands. He looked like a holy person so the man asked if he could become his disciple. The other said, 'You ask me to make you my disciple, but my problem is that my own guru has been missing for the past seven years and I don't know where he is. I have to seek his permission before I can make you my disciple.' He gave a description of his guru, adding that he went about bare-chested with just a cloth around his waist and a towel over his right shoulder, and that he was a great cook. The rich man realized that the description fitted that of his own cook, so he invited the other to return home with him.

When they reached the oasis, the door of the hut opened and the cook came out. The holy man immediately prostrated himself before him, crying, 'You were trying to teach him for seven years, and he's still looking for a guru!' The other replied, 'It took seven years for him to realize that he needed a guru, and he's still searching. Please make him your disciple. I have work to do and am leaving now.'

Since that is a Sufi tale, there are many angles to it.

Now we need jean-clad yogis.

161

Q: What's your message for the future?

If the youth can change, they will bring about a change in the future. To look at the future, one has to look at the present. It's like the karmic theory we have in India. You cannot go back and tinker with anything you have done in your life, and you don't really know what the future will bring. The only thing you have is the now. This is the time to work on that.

Technology is a good tool, and it is going to grow. We cannot return to village life. A hundred ago a hundred people could have attended a satsang. Today, one can reach two million people with the click of a button. With one tap on your phone app, you can get a great deal of information. It is a burden to carry unnecessary material in your head, especially if you are seeking something new, something which is fresh. If your mind is steady, you can use technology without being distracted.

Use technology as a tool to understand the inner self, consciousness, compassion. You can change things if you want. It's in your hands. Know that and understand it. I offer you this great hope.

In this busy world we have to work and perform, but do not let that busyness penetrate deep within your consciousness. Inside yourself, be pristine, be pure like the lotus. Do not become the external image of yourself.

Spirituality today has to be practiced in the middle of the noisy marketplace of jobs, jets, cars, commotions, anxieties, possessions, husbands, wives, children.

Sri M's Aphorisms

It's good to erase one's yesterdays and live in today. Then you are lighter; there are no burdens.

You have a slate and you write on it. Each time you write on it, if you want to write anything else, you first have to rub out the old stuff. So, in matters of inner exploration, the most important thing is to keep your slate clean.

It's more important to understand the teachings than to worship the teacher. The sacred is always around us and in our hearts.

Understand yourself. Everything that you need is in you. There is nothing outside. Be independent and wherever possible, be kind to others. What is spirituality? It is to find the truth, to find yourself, to find who you are, and what is your link with the Supreme Being.

Sharing is an essential part of well-being. As you give, so you receive. So, give whenever possible, whatever possible, in whichever way you can.

Don't unnecessarily complicate life with too many things. That does not mean that when you speak the truth you have to be blunt. There are sweet ways of speaking the truth.

Obsession conditions the mind; it doesn't free the mind. When the mind is free, it finds the answer in a flash. The answer comes from within.

When the mind is open, and when there is a great desire to achieve something, then the channels for achieving it are opened.

Write down your goal. Every night, before you go to sleep, take the slip, read it as many times as you can. Repeat it like a mantra. Put it under your pillow and go to sleep. Believe me, if you are serious and sacrifice your time and energy, the mind will find ways and means to bring about situations that will open up your future to fulfilling the aim. This is true. Imagination is a gift from the Divine.

True consciousness means to go beyond all images. Not images that you see around you but the images that we build up in our minds. It is because of these images that we get hurt.

If we live in this world with the heart anchored to the core Truth, then we can live more efficiently than ever before.

Unless something dies and disappears, there's no place for anything new to take birth.

The sacredness, the happiness, the vastness that you seek, the solution for the 'never-ending desires' that you seek, all this is already there with you, in you.

Once you touch it, even a little bit, even if you touch the hem of garment of Truth, then there is no more fear, there is no more anxiety, there is no more confusion in the mind.

ॐ असतो मा सद्गमय ।
तमसो मा ज्योतिर्गमय ।
मृत्योर्मा अमृतं गमय ।
ॐ शान्तिः शान्तिः शान्तिः ॥

asato mā sadgamaya
tamasomā jyotir gamaya
mrityormāamritam gamaya
Oṁ śhānti śhānti śhāntiḥ

Be simple. Throw off the burdens and be free
May I be lifted from Falsehood
into Truth
May I ascend from darkness
to light
May I soar from death to
deathlessness